Alan Bold was born in Edinburgh in 1943 and now lives with his wife and daughter in rural Fife. He has published many books of poetry including *To Find the New*, *A Perpetual Motion Machine*, *The State of the Nation* and *A Pint of Bitter* as well as a selection in *Penguin Modern Poets 15*. He has edited *The Penguin Book of Socialist Verse*, *The Martial Muse: Seven Centuries of War Poetry*, the *Cambridge Book of English Verse 1939–75*; and written critical books on *Thom Gunn & Ted Hughes*, *The Ballad* and *George Mackay Brown*. He is also active as a visual artist and has had many exhibitions of his Illuminated Poems (pictures combining an original poetic manuscript with an illustrative composition).

edited with an introduction by Alan Bold

Making Love

The Picador Book of Erotic Verse

published by Pan Books

First published 1978 by Pan Books Ltd,
Cavaye Place, London SW10 9PG
4th printing 1980
Introduction © Alan Bold 1978
Compilation © Pan Books 1978
ISBN 0 330 25585 1
Printed in Great Britain by
Richard Clay (The Chaucer Press) Ltd, Bungay, Suffolk

Contents

8

Introduction

Sex and poetry, to those prone to immaculate preconceptions, might seem strange bedfellows. In fact they make incredibly fertile partners, the private sensitivity of poetry effortlessly penetrating the public area of sexuality. For too long now poetry has been the possession of a tiny minority proud of belonging to an exclusive club. To the poet the public has appeared, in Milton's phrase, as 'A miscellaneous rabble, who extol / Things vulgar';* to the public the poet has seemed a disembodied voice whimpering in the wilderness. Moreover these fallacious assumptions have been assiduously encouraged by critics who, as self-appointed arbiters of literary taste, have been content to portray poetry as a largely irrelevant exercise in self-indulgence. Yet the problem is not without an obvious solution, for poets have not always been neglected nor has the public always been deprived of the felicities of poetry. Modern poets can learn from past masters of their craft to deal with subjects of crucial, not peripheral, concern and can make their work memorable by creating it with a combination of technical excellence and imaginative insight. The public will surely respond to poetry when it impinges on everyday affairs – like sex. And what could possibly interest the public more than sex? The fact that I have just posed a rhetorical question is itself evidence of the persistent human appeal of sex; or, to put it another way, the sex appeal of humanity. For ever since men and women became what they are, sex has been a central issue between them. Poetry, as I hope this anthology shows, has a unique contribution to make to the vast literature on sexual matters.

In a short poem composed in the 1590s, 'The Triple Fool', John Donne reflected on his habitual practice of recording his amorous exploits in verse:

> I am two fools, I know,
> For loving, and for saying so
>   In whining poetry

Now Donne's achievement as a lover was a matter for his female

* *Paradise Regained*, Book III, lines 50–51.

contemporaries to judge: posterity has certainly decided that his amatory poems, far from 'whining', display a sensuous subtlety that is the quintessence of great erotic art. Yet Donne's compulsive need to survey his sexual adventures in retrospect is typical of the confessional nature of most erotic poetry. Few lovers get much thanks from their partners for revealing the intimate details of a shared passion. Indeed, we have it on the authority of movie star Mae West that

Usually the men who spend the most time talking about sex never get around to doing it – and if they should be ready, their prospective partner is probably bored and long gone.*

There is, with deference to Miss West, a difference between sexual gossip and erotic poetry for the former is frequently unworthy of the sexual act while the latter artistically glorifies it.

Thus poets deserve praise for immortalizing precise sexual encounters. Motivated by an intense appreciation of fleshly delights erotic poets have through the ages erected intricate, enduring monuments to a basically spasmodic activity. They have given sex a poetic dimension of timelessness and allow us to contemplate it in all its aspects. The emotion might be recollected with more heavy breathing than tranquillity but all the better for that so long as artistic integrity is preserved. To their credit the poets have wielded their pens, like their penises, to give as well as to receive pleasure. By verbally perpetuating their own sexual experiences they have made a comparative art of love accessible to all. Of course, no one pretends that erotic poems are a substitute for sexual activism but they may stimulate love and make lovers more selective in their search for sensation.

In case potential lovers are discouraged by the apparent sexual infallibility of some erotic poets let us admit right away that not all of them were as good in bed as they were at describing pre- or post-coital acrobatics. Like everyone else they were always ambitious but not always adept. Donne, who gained an early reputation as 'a great visitor of ladies, a great frequenter of plays, a great writer of conceited verses' was certainly a womanizer in his youth and took personal risks by eloping with Ann More to whom most of his

* *Mae West on Sex, Health and ESP*, London 1975, p. 22.

sensual poems were addressed.* His masterly poetic utterances on love are urgent invitations to a lifetime of undercover bliss, yet after taking Holy Orders at the age of forty-three, Donne subsequently addressed himself to God rather than to women. Herrick, who was ordained in 1623, placed this apologetic couplet at the end of his sexually stimulating *Hesperides* (1648):

To his book's end this last line he'd have placed,
Jocund his muse was; but his life was chaste.

Baudelaire, perhaps the greatest nineteenth-century exponent of poetic eroticism, was an even more extreme case for, rather than portraying profound sexual knowledge, he took a voyeuristic delight at the sensuous spectacle of the female body. Enid Starkie accurately observed:

A study of the erotic poems of Baudelaire suggests the view that the most intense physical sensations he ever received were through the organs of sight, sensations amounting almost to orgasm.†

The photographer Nadar, a close friend, claimed in his *Baudelaire Intime* (1911) that the author of *Les Fleurs du Mal* ('Flowers of Evil') was a virgin and quoted Baudelaire's mulatto girlfriend Jeanne Duval as saying that the poet was 'a gentle inoffensive lunatic, whose passion spent itself in versifying.' So though 'erotic' is an epithet essential to Baudelaire's most intense poetry it might not have been applicable to the man.

Not all erotic poems written by men enlarge on their sexual prowess. There are also lamentations of impotence. Ovid's 'Either she was foul' (Elegy vii, Book III of the *Amores*) is the model for such poems and lines 123–42 of Nashe's 'The Choice of Valentines' paraphrase this elegy of Ovid's. Rochester's 'The Imperfect Enjoyment' is likewise a clever variant on the Ovidian original. Linked to these admissions of occasional impotence is the mock horror poets have expressed at the potential rivalry of the dildo. This subject is superbly handled by Nashe and hilariously deployed in Rochester's scandalous 'Signior Dildo'. The dildo is seen as an exotic invader: for Nashe it 'fortifies disdain with foreign arts', for

* In *The White Goddess*, London 1948, amended and enlarged edition 1952,
   p. 426, Robert Graves insisted that Ann More was Donne's 'only Muse'.
† Enid Starkie, *Baudelaire*, London 1957, Pelican edition p. 102.

Rochester it is a 'noble Italian'. A letter of 26 January 1670 from Henry Savile to Rochester tells of a box of imported dildoes being seized and burned by customs officers, so the poetic wish was father to the official act in this instance at least.

Sex is a notoriously difficult subject to discuss uninhibitedly and it is a triumph of poetry that though, when published, it becomes public property it still retains an element of dignified privacy. The relationship between artist and appreciator is, ideally, a one-to-one affair – like sex. For centuries poets have expressed their profound appreciation of the opposite sex in vivid verbal *tableaux* and readers of erotic poetry have been privileged to relive, albeit vicariously, acts that would otherwise have perished. Apart from the ingredient of privacy, poetry has other qualities in common with sex: both rely on rhythm; both can stand many repeat performances; both, at their best, are so memorable as to be unforgettable; both benefit from concentration and sustained technical virtuosity; both have a cerebral as well as a physical presence.

Although sex is the most fundamental fact of life – the *sine qua non* of human survival – it has usually been excluded from the permissible areas of public discussion. Nobody is surprised when a general or politician openly advocates war and destruction; for an individual to publicly proclaim love and procreation is considered offensive. Poetry shaped by the inspirational force of sexuality is generally immune from these socially convenient strictures. The poet's subversive assertion of the general significance of particular events may have made him something of a social outsider but it is to this outsider that informed people are attracted when they want confirmation of their individuality. Poetry reinforces the best instincts of humanity and poets have done much to win respect for the complexities of sex. They have transformed the act of love from a rut-and-gut affair to something infinitely precious. At various times, when sex has been relegated to the realms of absolute secrecy, poets have reminded their readers that the flesh exists as a beautifully inescapable feature of human intercourse.

That the poets have won (or been permitted to win) this battle to gain a victorious appreciation of sexuality is shown by the changing status of erotic poetry. In AD8 the Emperor Augustus banished Ovid from Rome to lifelong exile in Tomis, an outpost on the Black Sea. Although he may have had embarrassing inside knowledge of an affair involving Augustus's daughter Julia (also exiled) Ovid's principal crime was the publication of his *Ars Amatoria* ('The Art of Love'). In June 1599 Christopher Marlowe's translations of Ovid were burned by order of the Church of England. Tolerance of sexual honesty is a test of the civilized society and it is fascinating to see how various administrations have responded to erotic poetry. On 20 August 1857, almost two months after the appearance of *Les Fleurs du Mal*, Charles Baudelaire appeared at a police court in Paris on a charge of offending public morality for which crime he was fined 300 francs (later reduced to 50 francs) and prevented from publishing six of the poems. This ban was not officially reversed in France until 31 May 1949.

Baudelaire's treatment was hardly of Ovidian proportions and elsewhere things were gradually changing. John Hayward's 1926 edition of Rochester's poems came out in a limited edition in Britain and was destroyed by the New York authorities, while Graham Greene found the moral climate of the 1930s so coy that he could not persuade his publisher to accept his life of Rochester.* However, on 14 March 1934 the BBC magazine *The Listener* published Dylan Thomas's 'Light breaks where no sun shines' and after a barrage of complaints about the poem's apparent obscenity all that happened was that a public apology was issued. This could not deter other poets from publishing erotica and eventually a liberal attitude has prevailed. Either officialdom has become increasingly unconcerned with poetry because its minority status makes it an unworthy subject of persecution; or the right of the serious artist to choose his own subject has been recognized. It would be nice to accept the latter reason – nice but proabably naïve.

In the epilogue to 'The Choice of Valentines' – dedicated to Ferdinando Stanley, Lord Strange – Thomas Nashe invoked 'Ovid's wanton muse' and called Ovid himself 'the fountain whence my streams do flow'. Marlowe and Dryden translated Ovid, and Matthew Prior said in verses 'Written in an Ovid':

Ovid is the surest guide,
    You can name, to show the way
To any woman, maid, or bride,
    Who resolves to go astray.

* See Graham Greene's Preface to his *Lord Rochester's Monkey*, London 1974, p. 9.

Ovid is the erotic poet *par excellence*. His poetry is didactic: he speaks as a master of the art of love seeking to initiate novices into the mysteries of sex. For all his frankness, though, Ovid is never coarse. As Dryden wrote in his Preface of 1680 to Ovid's *Epistles* 'no man has ever treated the passion of love with so much delicacy of thought, and of expression, or searched into the nature of it more philosophically than he.' This relates to the fact that there are two distinct traditions of erotic poetry. There are sophisticated poems written by professional poets like Ovid and Donne and Baudelaire; and there are salacious poems generally written by anonymous amateurs who, spellbound by a single theme, literally rise to the occasion. Much of the salacious verse has enjoyed an underground existence, has been orally transmitted before being textually frozen by collectors like Burns in *The Merry Muses of Caledonia*. This anthology represents both traditions – the elegantly erotic and the basically bawdy – and it would be a mistake to seek too much qualitative differences between them. While there are few amateurs who could aspire to the metaphorical density of Donne there are few professional poets who could match the panache of a modern classic like 'Eskimo Nell'.

Clearly eroticism predates poetry and many amatory poems reach back into antique cultures: when they do so they tend to support the view that sexual behaviour has remained fairly consistent. The biblical 'Song of Songs' is stylistically an encomium, a formal hymn to physical beauty, though the context is marital. 'Daphnis', the pastoral dialogue by Theocritus, is chronologically old but modern enough in its mood. It even anticipates the contemporary literary interest in the hypergamous marriage for the girl seeking to barter her favours for a solid marriage proposal and makes the point:

Your kindred is not much amiss, 'tis true,
Yet I am somewhat better born than you.

In this poem, as in others like Edward Moore's 'Fable', marriage is seen, often comically, as the beginning of domestic love and the end of passionate sex. And in erotic poetry, as in tennis, the proclamation of love can stand for nothing. As a distinct species the male writer usually wants to have his cake and at least a few crumbs of comfort on the side, so while he is drawn to the convenience of marriage he is likely to forever long for fresh fields and pastures new. Thurber, in his infinite wisdom, put it this way:

A writer's wife usually lasts until her husband begins addressing her by snapping his fingers or going 'Psst!' This is an invariable sign that he is going through what we call change of wife in the male. In such a state the writer husband often uses expressions like 'marry-go-round' and 'welded blitz'.*

It is true of erotic poetry, as of poetry generally, that most of the practitioners are male (though by almost ending on three contributions by women this anthology shows how things are changing). Thus the object of desire is female – at least in a heterosexual collection like this – and women may raise the usual objections to the male's imperious attitude to women. By far the majority of erotic poems dwell on the physical beauty of women, endorsing Browning's statement:

God's best of beauteous and magnificent
Revealed to earth – the naked female form.†

Yes, the physical pleasure associated with female nudity permeates the best erotic poetry. It is one of the contentions of the Women's Liberation Movement that it is actually degrading for a female to be treated as a sex-object but if men are sexually objective it corresponds to sexual subjectivity in women. To insist that women disguise their sexual magic in the interests of some feminist theory is to substitute polemic for common sensuality. The fascination with the female form is natural to men and much of the impetus of institutional Women's Liberation is provided by socially privileged females in search of a fashionable topic of discussion – 'the lady doth protest too much, methinks' as Queen Gertrude says in Hamlet (III. ii. 242). It is an interesting irony apparently overlooked by the most publicity-conscious feminists that when they shortened the name of their movement to Women's Lib they revealed more than a slogan: for the verb lib (from the Dutch lubben) means to geld. I wonder how many women would like to march under the banner of Women's Geld?

One of the leading spokeswomen of the feminist movement,

* James Thurber, Vintage Thurber, vol. II, London 1963, p. 499.
† Robert Browning, 'Parleyings With Certain People: Francis Furini' (1887).

Germaine Greer, has firmly downgraded the sexually provocative appeal of breasts:

A full bosom is actually a millstone around a woman's neck: it endears her to the men who want to make their mammet of her, but she is never allowed to think that their popping eyes actually see her ... [breasts] are not parts of a person but lures slung around her neck, to be kneaded and twisted like magic putty, or mumbled and mouthed like lolly ices.*

The short answer to this would be: *balls!* Not only are breasts very much part of a person – and appreciated as such – but breast-worship has a respectable physiological origin. When, in a massive evolutionary erection, man (and woman) stood upright the hitherto irresistible female backside was obscured in frontal contact so that breasts evolved as a visually attractive substitute for the buttocks. Desmond Morris – like Germaine Greer a bestselling chart-topper – has convincingly established this:

If the female of our species was going to successfully shift the interest of the male round to the front, evolution would have to do something to make the frontal region more stimulating. At some point, back in our ancestry, we must have been using the rear approach ... Can we, if we look at the frontal regions of the females of our species, see any structures that might possibly be mimics of the ancient genital display of hemispherical buttocks and red labia? The answer stands out as clearly as the female bosom itself. The protuberant, hemispherical breasts of the female must surely be copies of the fleshly buttocks, and the sharply defined red lips around the mouth must be copies of the red labia.†

In his poem 'Foursome' Paul Verlaine intuitively grasped this zoological point when he called the buttocks 'big sisters of the breasts'.

Erotic poetry abounds in figurative allusions to the breasts. In D. H. Lawrence's 'Gloire de Dijon'‡ they are likened to full-bloom roses; in MacDiarmid's 'O Wha's the Bride' the lady has 'briests like stars'; Neruda's 'Lone Gentleman' sees 'women's breasts shining like eyes'. Cunt-worship is not so frequently verbalized as breast-worship but is evoked in many similes that seek to convey images of infinity. The cunt is usually imagined as a profound well or

* Germaine Greer, *The Female Eunuch*, London 1970, Paladin edition p. 34.
† Desmond Morris, *The Naked Ape*, London 1967, p. 499.
‡ Sadly, permission to include Lawrence in this anthology was refused.

delicious fountain. Nashe, in 'The Choice of Valentines', compared the belly to

the bending of a hill
At whose decline a fountain dwelleth still

while the anonymous seventeenth-century poem 'Last night I dreamed' ends

Her belly's like to yonder hill –
Some call it Mount of Pleasure –
And underneath there springs a well
Which no man's depth can measure.

A more literary concept is the image of the cunt as a 'two-leaved book' in the seventeenth-century poem 'A Riddle' and the eighteenth-century 'The Maid's Conjuring Book' where

She opened wide her conjuring book,
And laid the leaves at large.

And of course, there is Donne's celebrated geographical exclamation: 'O my America!' The whole style of erotic poetry depends on verbal images for the female anatomy (and, less often, the male anatomy). At its finest this linguistic striptease gives rise to major poetry as in the case of Donne; at its crudest the method is too rude to be truly poetic but results in vigorous verse like the anonymous twentieth-century 'That Portion of a Woman'.

The rhythm of sex itself is often given a musical connotation: in Nashe's 'The Choice of Valentines' the lovers keep 'crotchet-time',

Whilst she, that had preserved me by her pity,
Unto our music framed a groaning ditty.

The anonymous seventeenth-century 'Upon a Courtesan's Lute' alludes to the lady's 'instrument' while the conceit is repeated a century later in 'The Wanton Trick' where 'A pleasant young maid on an instrument played.' In many of the orally transmitted rural songs sex is portrayed in terms of agricultural ritual and it is easy to see how the plough penetrating the earth with seed could have a sexual significance. As agriculture became more mechanized so did rural eroticism as we can see in 'The Thrashing Machine'.

Metaphorical invention is, indeed, the hallmark of erotic verse, for as the Cavalier poet Alexander Brome wrote in 'The Resolve':

The glories of your ladies be
   But metaphors of things;
And but resemble what we see
   Each common object brings.

Another stylistic feature of erotic poetry is the reliance on euphemism. This is not always utilized out of prudery or a fear of censorship. It can also enchant the reader with its own conventions, because it depends on audience participation. We are all familiar with the comedian whose ostensibly innocent patter carries strong sexual overtones. 'I have a longstanding problem with my credentials,' he will say and the audience supply the sexual implications. A similar way of playing on human sexuality is seen in the twentieth-century poems 'Susanna' and 'A Blue Sea Romance' where the absence of obvious rhymes is strongly suggestive. In more sophisticated verse the favourite device is the use of 'dying' as a synonym for orgasm. Dryden's 'A New Song' employs this euphemism which is fully stated in the poem 'Desired Death' from *Madrigals and Epigrams* (1616) by William Drummond of Hawthorden:

Dear life while as I touch
These coral ports of bliss,
Which still themselves do kiss,
And sweetly me invite to do as much,
All parting in my lips,
My life my heart doth leave,
No sense my senses have,
And inward powers do find a strange eclipse,
This death so heavenly well
Doth so me please, that I
Would never longer seek in sense to dwell,
If that even thus I only could but die.

The dying/orgasm equation still has some popularity as a deliberately anachronistic detail. Robert Graves, in 'Down, Wanton, Down!' addresses the wanton penis:

Indifferent what you storm or why,
So be that in the breech you die!

Related to the orgasmic death is the martial symbolism of sex as a battlefield contested by two antagonists. Herrick, in 'On Love', put the matter succinctly:

Love is a kind of war; hence those who fear,
No cowards must his royal ensigns bear.

The symbolism is inevitable: seduction becomes a prelude to conquest, and the penis is the ultimate weapon. In a stridently feminist book which holds that man is genetically inferior to woman – 'man is but an imperfect female' (p. 34) – Elizabeth Gould Davis launched an attack on the quality of this weapon:

The penis is the only muscle man has that he cannot flex. It is also the only extremity he cannot control . . . But even worse, as it affects the dignity of its owner, is its seeming obedience to that inferior thing, woman. It rises at the sight, or even at the thought, of a woman.*

Again, this is something that has been determined by the exigencies of cultural evolution for it would be awkward, to say the least, for men to have an erect penis at all times. The sexually arousing presence of women is designed to get it ready for action. The only men who actually resent the functional erection are misogynists and they would have little place in an anthology of erotic poetry were it not for the paradoxical fact that misogynism has resulted in a special type of erotic poetry which is sexual in spite of itself.

In his provocative preface to *Getting Married II* (published in October 1886) August Strindberg wrote:

Woman invented the idea that she should be paid for her favours. As a prostitute she is paid per time, as a married woman by contract. It comes to the same thing. By appearing to be reluctant she excites man's passions to the point of madness, which finds an outlet in woman-worship and erotic poetry, by means of which man has lived right up to the present time in a blissful state of self-deception about his humiliation, the true nature of woman, and her dominant position.

Why is it that there is not in the literature of any country a hymn of

* Elizabeth Gould Davis, *The First Sex*, London 1973, Penguin edition p. 152.

praise to man written by a woman? Because she must of necessity despise her dupe.*

Strindberg's misogynism was by no means unique: great international culture-heroes like Tolstoy and Ghandi came to believe that sexual passion was somehow shameful, that for a man to succumb to his desire for a woman was unmanly. Otto Weininger, the German writer, was convinced that physical contact with women contaminated man's intrinsic spirituality. His *Geschlecht und Charakter* ('Sex and Character') went through twenty editions from 1903–23 and by 1923 had been translated into eight languages. The rationale that leads men to take up misogynism as a private crusade was even conceded by a woman, Esther Vilar, who wrote in almost Strindbergian terms:

By the age of twelve at the latest, most women have decided to become prostitutes. Or, to put it another way, they have planned a future for themselves which consists of choosing a man and letting him do all the work. In return for his support they are prepared to let him make use of their vagina at certain given moments. The minute a woman has taken this decision she ceases to develop her mind.†

These allegedly predatory attributes of women have been seized on by some poets. In Book IV of his *De Rerum Natura* – a poetic exposition of Epicurean philosophy – Lucretius describes the mentally unsettling consequences of physical passion and implicitly acknowledges its attraction. Juvenal's Sixth Satire is an extraordinary misogynistic outburst and in his introduction to his magnificent translation of it John Dryden sensibly put the matter in perspective:

this [i.e. the Sixth Satire] he reserved wholly for the ladies. How they had offended him I know not: but upon the whole matter he is not to be excused for imputing to all, the vices of some few amongst them. Neither was it generously done of him, to attack the weakest as well as the fairest part of the creation: neither do I know what moral he could reasonably draw from it. It could not be to avoid the whole sex, if all had been true which he alleges against them: for that had been to put an end of human kind. And to bid us beware of their artifices, is a kind of silent acknowledgement, that they have more wit than men: which turns the

* August Strindberg, *Getting Married*, trans. Mary Sandbach, London 1972, Quartet edition p. 197.
† Esther Vilar, *The Manipulated Man*, tr Eva Borneman, London 1971, p. 19.

satire upon us, and particularly upon the poet; who thereby makes a compliment where he means a libel.

It would hardly be expected that women would find misogynistic poems either erotic or apt. More pleasing to the ladies is the tradition of courtly love that has had such a pervasive influence on literature. This literary convention was perfected in eleventh-century France by the troubadours. It is an aristocratic genre that elevates the rich lady to quasi-religious divinity. Undoubtedly the courtly rules of love contained an element of masochism, for the poet's most persistent posture is one of total submission to his capricious goddess. She is beautiful and unattainable; the poet sighs for an adulterous relationship with her. In erotic poems which depend on a voyeuristic adoration of the female form there are vestiges of the courtly tradition but most erotic poems consciously react against *amour courtois* by making women eminently touchable and willing. The salacious poems that have been orally transmitted completely reverse the method of the troubadours by portraying women as not only the instigators of sexual intercourse but the real sexual experts (see, for example, 'Eskimo Nell').

In the intellectual climate of the nineteenth century it was thought necessary for self-appointed sages to formulate exclusive, universally applicable theories to explain the inner drive that motivates human behaviour. For Darwin it was the physiological struggle for survival; for Marx (who wanted to dedicate *Das Kapital* to Darwin) it was economic necessity; for Nietzsche it was the will to power; for Sigmund Freud it was sexuality. In the relatively affluent West the dominant influence has been that of Freud who, for all his theoretical absurdities and often spurious premises, did much to introduce a healthy honesty into sexual discussions. In America Freudian psychoanalysts have become the new priesthood giving human confessions the expensive benefit of their free association. In empirical Britain, largely conditioned by the ubiquitous presence of subliminal advertising, our everyday iconography has become so Freudian that we tend to see the material world as a mass of phallic and vaginal symbols. However, an even greater influence on our conceptual habits has been exerted by Plato who maintained that earthly objects are imperfect copies of abstract ideals. A. N. Whitehead thought Western philosophy comprised no more than a series of footnotes to Plato and it is true that, while we reject so-called Platonic love, we constantly visualize objects (including sex objects) in a Platonic manner. Whether this was because of astounding philosophical perspicacity on Plato's part or whether some two thousand years ago he elucidated the obvious ('What oft was thought but ne'er so well expressed' as Pope's *An Essay on Criticism* has it) is beside the point. What is important is our Platonic vision of the opposite sex. The ideal woman is a flawless goddess whether she appears in a poem or a painting or the centrefold of a girlie magazine. We measure mortal women by immortal standards and many of the women who feature in erotic poems display an unearthly perfection. There is a corollary though, for other erotic poems are totally realistic in their treatment of sexuality as it manifests itself in reality, not dreams.

I have tried to present, in this book, the dreams and the reality, the sophisticated and the salacious, the beautiful and the basic. I have also attempted to show the international range of eroticism though, naturally, I have attached major importance to poems in English. In Britain there has been a strong element of eroticism in all periods of poetry. Chaucer, who has been accused of fathering English poetry, set an erotic precedent in the person of his Wife of Bath. Spenser, Shakespeare and Nashe elaborated on erotic details and the indigenous tradition came to a climax in the seventeenth century with Donne, Herrick, Carew, Marvell and a whole host of anonymous bards. Herrick was a foot-fetishist to whom a glimpse of ankle or even a shoe was a prelude to ecstasy. In that superb poem 'The Description of a Woman' we see him at his most voyeuristic, dwelling on every aspect of femininity beginning at the head and ending, appropriately, at the feet. Carew's 'A Rapture' is more dynamic than anything by Herrick but by this time the worship of women had reached such a poetic pinnacle that Suckling, in 'The Deformed Mistress', could offer a paradoxical encomium and still be erotic. Much of the anonymous seventeenth-century work appeared in drolleries – ribald anthologies – until Cromwellian puritanism decided to put a stop to them. Milton, who had championed unlicensed printing in *Areopagitica* (1644), became Latin Secretary in Cromwell's censorious government. On 25 April 1656 a drollery, *Sportive Wit* (from which the poem 'Love's Courtship' is taken) compiled by Milton's nephew John Philips, was condemned as 'scandalous' and burned by the hangman; two weeks later another book, *Choyce Drollery*, suffered the same fate. No more ribaldry appeared openly until after the Restoration when eroticism again reared its lovely head and the great Rochester became first in the field.

In the eighteenth century England's poets were more inclined to morality than immorality and the pieces by Swift and Pope included here are examples of ethical eroticism rather than the real thing; however, eighteenth-century Scotland produced a great bawdy poet and collector of bawdry in Robert Burns. It was the Victorian era that really suppressed the erotic. Officially the established attitude to sex was a domestic application of courtly love; in *Adam Bede* (1859) George Eliot (Mary Anne Evans) expressed herself in terms that would have delighted a medieval troubadour:

He was but three-and-twenty, and had only just learned what it is to love – love with that adoration which a young man gives to a woman whom he feels to be greater and better than himself. Love of this sort is hardly distinguishable from religious feeling. What deep and worthy love is not so?

A book by Eric Trudgill, whose ingenious title distinguishes between *Madonnas and Magdalens*, shows that while respectable Victorian literature exalted the pure virginal untouchable image of womanhood, the darker corners of Victorian life were illuminated by the delights of the prostitute. The split between domestic lie-back-and-think-of-England asexuality and surreptitious depravity put women in an impossible either/or position – they were either angels or diabolical temptresses and never the twain shall meet:

If the home was to be the place of peace and the fount of civic virtues, it was essential both to banish fallen women from society lest they contaminate by example and temptation, and to make them bear the stigma of public obloquy.*

Gladstone, grand old man that he was, used to go to the aid of London prostitutes though apparently his interest was confined to the attractive ones.

Although we still sometimes suffer from a hangover of Victorian hypocrisy, sexual honesty has increased since those days. Sex is now almost a religion replacing the established religions. It is not surprising that there is little coexistence between eroticism and

* Eric Trudgill, *Madonnas and Magdalens*, London 1976, p. 13.

professional piety because the various ecclesiastical institutions have offered the individual the reward of insubstantial spirituality when he or she longs for a substantial body. Presbyterianism rejected the flesh as a wicked ornament and saw extramarital intercourse opening a trapdoor to hell. Catholicism found itself in a peculiar position for on the one hand it encouraged fecundity and on the other it eulogized two sexually unproductive figures, the virgin mother (Mary) and the celibate father (pope = Latin *papa* = father). As for the familiar *via media* of the Anglican church, its eschewal of extremism promoted the apotheosis of apathy.

Today eroticism has greatly benefited from the lifting of restrictions on publishing. It has been a slow, but satisfying process. A poem by Hugh MacDiarmid, 'Ode to All Rebels', which referred to

the great Discovery of the Age
– That women like It too!

was actually deleted from the first edition of *Stony Limits and Other Poems* (1934). Now we need no longer pretend we prefer verbal virginity to vigour and can sympathize with W. H. Auden when he says 'I prefer the comic or the coarse note to the hot-and-bothered or the whining-pathetic.'[*] At last, as this anthology shows, it is possible to present the whole glorious range of poetic erotica in the hope that it will delight and instruct a tolerant public. For surely there is a place for eroticism in the life of every man and woman. It is a salutary influence on life and a great artistic presence, for D. H. Lawrence was right when he said in 1929 that 'Half the great poems, pictures, music, stories of the whole world are great by virtue of their sex appeal.'[†]

Until recently scholars have been reluctant to admit the erotic element and when they haven't shied away from the subject they have glossed over it with some embarrassment. In his otherwise excellent study of Thomas Nashe, G. R. Hibbard said of 'The Choice of Valentines':

Viewed as a work of art it adds nothing to his literary stature. The story it tells has no real point and part of it is downright silly ... Valueless as poetry.[‡]

[*] W. H. Auden, *A Certain World* London 1971, p. 230.
[†] D. H. Lawrence, *A Propos of Lady Chatterley's Lover*, Harmondsworth 1961, p. 65.
[‡] G. R. Hibbard, *Thomas Nashe*, London 1962, p. 57.

That shows how solemnity vitiates appreciation, for the poem deserves to be resuscitated as one of the finest bawdy poems in the English language. It moves with a grand, and appropriate, rhythmic energy and has many excellent images in it as when, lamenting his lack of sexual potency, Nashe produces a witty, telling classical allusion:

I am not as was Hercules the stout,
That to the seventh journey could hold out.

That kind of ability to be at ease with sexuality is one of the most liberating features of erotic poetry and it is time more people were aware of it.

No anthology pleases everybody but I hope this one reaches the general public as well as serious students of poetry (as long as they are not serious *all* the time). For future editions I will be interested to receive any hitherto unpublished treasures of orally transmitted erotica, and can be reached via the publisher. For the moment I rest my case on the following poems themselves. I believe this book will interest everyone with an interest in the erotic and that must surely constitute a majority. I hope, too, the book will readily exhibit its own intrinsic appeal and that it might even exert a seminal influence on future generations.

Alan Bold

Archilochus

circa 680–circa 640BC

Epode

'. . . keeping your hands right off.
   Best to try for a love that's returned –

And if you're impatient, if your heart drives you forward,
   There's somebody here in our house
     Is out of her mind for you:

A delicate, sweet young girl – and, the way I see her,
   Flawless, just perfect. It's true
     You've made her unhappy: but still—'

Such were her words, and this the answer I gave her:
   'Daughter of Amphimedo –
     That noble lady of blessed

Memory, tucked away now in the dank earth's clasp –
   Young men know many delights
     Of the Love-goddess, quite apart

From that sacred affair: one such can serve our needs.
   These matters will you and I
     Discuss at our leisure when

Darkness draws down, the two of us together.
   Spare you I will, as you ask,
     Consumed though I am with desire:

Ah, let me creep under your fence, pass in through the wicket –
   Sweetheart, don't grudge me that:
     I'll stay outside on the lawn

In the garden. And get this clear: Neobule's[1] finished
   For me. Any man who wants
     Can have her – she's ripe fruit now,

The bloom of her maidenhead faded, vanished away
   The charm she used to possess:
     Silly bitch, she could never say *No*,

An object-lesson in Not Overstepping The Limits,
    Strictly, now, for the birds.
        May sweet God in heaven never

Stick me with such a woman for wife, to make me
    A neighbourhood laughing-stock!
        Ah darling, it's you I want –

You're never disloyal or double-dealing. It's she
    Who's too sharp for my comfort, makes
        More friends than are healthy. I'm scared

What may come if I crowd and bed her – the bitch in the proverb
    Dropping her children blind
        Or before their proper time.'

So much I said, then took the girl's hand and laid her
    Down in a riot of flowers
        With a soft cloak as coverlet,

Cradling her neck in the crook of my arm, and soothed
    The fear that sprang to her eyes,
        The eyes of a startled fawn,

Caressing her breasts with my hands, but gently, gently,
    A soft assault to reveal
        The sweet flesh of her youth,

And embraced her beautiful body, touched it all over,
    And let the white strength of me come
        While stroking her yellow hair.

Anonymous

4th century BC

from *The Song of Songs* (Canto II)

He

How charming you are, beloved!
　　How meet for the pleasures of love!
Your tallness suggests the palm tree
　　With your breasts its clusters of dates.
Said I, 'I must climb this palm tree,
　　And grasp its graceful branches.'
Your breasts will be as vine clusters,
　　The bouquet of your breath as quinces,
The taste of you like finest wine
　　That slides down the gullet smoothly,
Gliding over the lips and teeth.

She

I belong to my beloved.
　　His desire is for me alone.

Come away, then, my beloved!
　　Let us go into the country,
Lodge in one of the villages,
　　And start at dawn for the vineyards,
To see if the vines have budded,
　　Their blossoms begun to open,
And the pomegranates are in bloom.
　　There I will give you my love.

The love-apples send forth their fragrance
　　And at hand are all luscious fruits,
New ones as well as the old ones,
　　All destined for you, beloved.

Theocritus
circa 310–circa 250BC

Daphnis (Idyll 27)

Daphnis The shepherd Paris bore the Spartan bride
        By force away, and then by force enjoyed;
        But I by free consent can boast a bliss,
        A fairer Helen, and a sweeter kiss.

Chloris Kisses are empty joys and soon are o're.

Daphnis A kiss betwixt the lips is something more.

Chloris I wipe my mouth, and where's your kissing then?

Daphnis I swear you wipe it to be kissed again.

Chloris Go tend your herd, and kiss your cows at home;
        I am a maid, and in my beauty's bloom.

Daphnis 'Tis well remembered, do not waste your time;
        But wisely use it e're you pass your prime.

Chloris Blown roses hold their sweetness to the last,
        And raisins keep their luscious native taste.

Daphnis The sun's too hot; these olive shades are near;
        I fain would whisper something in your ear.

Chloris 'Tis honest talking where we may be seen,
        God knows that secret mischief you may mean;
        I doubt you'll play the wag and kiss again.

Daphnis At least beneath yon elm you need not fear;
        My pipe's in tune, if you're disposed to hear.

Chloris Play by yourself, I dare not venture thither:
        You, and your naughty pipe go hang together.

Daphnis Coy nymph beware, lest Venus you offend.

Chloris I shall have chaste Diana still to friend.

Daphnis You have a soul, and Cupid has a dart.

Chloris Diana will defend, or heal my heart.
        Nay, fie what mean you in this open place?
        Unhand me, or, I swear, I'll scratch your face.
        Let go for shame; you make me mad for spite;
        My mouth's my own; and if you kiss I'll bite.

Daphnis Away with your dissembling female tricks:
        What, would you 'scape the fate of all your sex?

Chloris I swear I'll keep my maidenhead till death,

And die as pure as Queen Elizabeth.

Daphnis Nay mum for that; but let me lay thee down;
Better with me, than with some nauseous clown.

Chloris I'd have you know, if I were so inclined,
I have been wooed by many a wealthy hind;
But never found a husband to my mind.

Daphnis But they are absent all; and I am here.

Chloris The matrimonial yoke is hard to bear;
And marriage is a woeful word to hear.

Daphnis A scarecrow, set to frighten fools away;
Marriage has joys; and you shall have a say.

Chloris Sour sauce is often mixed with our delight,
You kick by day more than you kiss by night.

Daphnis Sham stories all; but say the worst you can,
A very wife fears neither God nor Man.

Chloris But childbirth is they say, a deadly pain;
It costs at least a month to knit again.

Daphnis Diana cures the wounds Lucina[2] made;
Your goddess is a midwife by her trade.

Chloris But I shall spoil my beauty if I bear.

Daphnis But Mam and Dad are pretty names to hear.

Chloris But there's a civil question used of late;
Where lies my jointure, where your own estate?

Daphnis My flocks, my fields, my wood, my pastures take,
With settlement as good as law can make.

Chloris Swear then you will not leave me on the common,
But marry me, and make an honest woman.

Daphnis I swear by Pan (though he wears horns you'll say)
Cudgelled and kicked, I'll not be forced away.

Chloris I bargain for a wedding bed at least,
A house, and handsome lodging for a guest.

Daphnis A house well furnished shall be thine to keep;
And for a flock-bed I can shear my sheep.

Chloris What tale shall I to my old father tell?

Daphnis 'Twill make him chuckle thou'rt bestowed so well.

Chloris But after all, in troth I am to blame
To be so loving e're I know your name.
A pleasant sounding name's a pretty thing.

Daphnis Faith, mine's a very pretty name to sing;

They call me Daphnis: Lycidas my sire,
Nomaea bore me; farmers in degree,
He a good husband, a good housewife she.

Chloris Your kindred is not much amiss, 'tis true,
Yet I am somewhat better born than you.

Daphnis I know your father, and his family;
And without boasting am as good as he:
Menalcas; and no master goes before.

Chloris Hang both our pedigrees; not one word more;
But if you love me let me see your living,
Your house and home; for seeing is believing.

Daphnis See first yon cypress grove, (a shade from noon).
Chloris Browse on my goats; for I'll be with you soon.
Daphnis Feed well my bulls, to whet your appetite;
That each may take a lusty leap at night.

Chloris What do you mean (uncivil as you are),
To touch my breasts, and leave my bosom bare?

Daphnis These pretty bubbies first I make my own.
Chloris Pull out your hand, I swear, or I shall swoon.
Daphnis Why does the ebbing blood forsake thy face?
Chloris Throw me at least upon a cleaner place:
My linen ruffled, and my waistcoat soiling,
What, do you think new clothes were made for spoiling.

Daphnis I'll lay my lambskins underneath thy back.
Chloris My headgear's off; what filthy work you make!
Daphnis To Venus first, I lay these offerings by.
Chloris Nay first look round, that nobody be nigh:
Methinks I hear a whispering in the grove.

Daphnis The cypress trees are telling tales of love.
Chloris You tear off all behind me, and before me;
And I'm as naked as my mother bore me.

Daphnis I'll buy thee better clothes than these I tear,
And lie so close, I'll cover thee from air.

Chloris Y'are liberal now; but when your turn is sped,
You'll wish me choked with every crust of bread.

Daphnis I'll give thee more, much more than I have told;
Would I could coin my very heart to gold.

Chloris Forgive thy handmaid (huntress of the wood),
I see there's no resisting flesh and blood!

Daphnis	The noble deed is done; my herds I'll cull;
	Cupid, be thine a calf; and Venus, thine a bull.
Chloris	A maid I came, in an unlucky hour,
	But hence return, without my virgin flower.
Daphnis	A maid is but a barren name at best;
	If thou canst hold, I bid for twins at least.

    Thus did this happy pair their love dispense
With mutual joys, and gratified their sense;
The god of love was there a bidden guest;
And present at his own mysterious feast.
His azure mantle underneath he spread,
And scattered roses on the nuptial bed;
While folded in each other's arms they lay,
He blew the flames, and furnished out the play,
And from their foreheads wiped the balmy sweat away.
First rose the maid and with a glowing face,
Her downcast eyes beheld her print upon the grass;
Thence to her herd she sped herself in haste:
The bridegroom started from his trance at last,
And piping homeward jocundly he passed.

Lucretius
circa 95–circa 55BC

'*When love its utmost vigour*' (from *De Rerum Natura*, Book IV)

When love its utmost vigour does employ,
Ev'n then, 'tis but a restless wandering joy:
Nor knows the lover, in that wild excess,
With hands or eyes, what first he would possess:
But strains at all; and fastening where he strains,
Too closely presses with his frantic pains:
With biting kisses hurts the twining fair,
Which shows his joys imperfect, unsincere:
For stung with inward rage, he flings around,
And strives t'avenge the smart on that which gave the wound.

But love those eager bitings does restrain,
And mingling pleasure mollifies the pain.
For ardent hope still flatters anxious grief,
And sends him to his foe to seek relief:
Which yet the nature of the thing denies;
For love, and love alone of all our joys
By full possession does but fan the fire,
The more we still enjoy, the more we still desire.
Nature for meat, and drink provides a space;
And when received they fill a certain place;
Hence thirst and hunger may be satisfied,
But this repletion is to love denied:
Form, feature, colour, whatsoe're delight
Provokes the lovers' endless appetite,
These fill no space, nor can we thence remove
With lips, or hands, or all our instruments of love:
In our deluded grasp we nothing find,
But thin aerial shapes, that fleet before the mind.
As he who in a dream with drought is cursed,
And finds no real drink to quench his thirst,
Runs to imagined lakes his heat to steep,
And vainly swills and labours in his sleep;
So love with phantoms cheats our longing eyes,
Which hourly seeing never satisfies;
Our hands pull nothing from the parts they strain,
But wander o're the lovely limbs in vain:
Nor when the youthful pair more closely join,
When hands in hands they lock, and thighs in thighs they twine
Just in the raging foam of full desire,
When both press on, both murmur, both expire,
They gripe, they squeeze, their humid tongues they dart,
As each would force their way to t'other's heart:
In vain; they only cruise about the coast,
For bodies cannot pierce, nor be in bodies lost:
As sure they strive to be, when both engage,
In that tumultuous momentary rage,
So 'tangled in the nets of love they lie,
Till man dissolves in that excess of joy.
Then, when the gathered bag has burst its way,

And ebbing tides the slackened nerves betray,
A pause ensues; and nature nods a while,
Till with recruited rage new spirits boil;
And then the same vain violence returns,
With flames renewed th'erected furnace burns.
Again they in each other would be lost,
But still by adamantine bars are crossed;
All ways they try, successless all they prove,
To cure the secret sore of lingering love.

Catullus
circa 84–circa 54BC

'*Dear Ipsitilla*'

Dear Ipstilla, my sweetheart,
My darling, precious, beautiful tart,
Invite me round to be your guest
At noon. Say yes, and I'll request
Another favour: make quite sure
That no one latches the front door,
And don't slip out for a breath of air,
But stay inside, please, and prepare
A love-play with nine long acts in it,
No intervals either! Quick, this minute,
Now, if you're in the giving mood;
For lying here, full of good food,
I feel a second hunger poke
Up through my tunic and my cloak.

'*Cato*[3], *it's ludicrous*'

Cato, it's ludicrous, too absurd!
Do listen, it's worth chuckling over.
If you hold Catullus in affection,
Laugh, Cato, for what's just occurred

It's the funniest thing you've ever heard.
I caught a tender little lover,
Bottom up, rogering his bird,
And, brandishing my own erection
(Venus forgive me!), made a third.

'*The Lesbia*'[4]

The Lesbia, Caelius, whom in other days
Catullus loved, his great and only love,
My Lesbia, the girl I put above
My own self and my nearest, dearest ones,
Now hangs about crossroads and alleyways
Milking the cocks of mighty Remus' sons.

Meleager
1st century BC

'*Helen, who's in love*'

Helen, who's in love with love,
whose eyes are blue as seas offshore
from Paradise, persuades all men
to ride her depths with dripping oar.

Philodemus
1st century BC

'*At sixty*'

At sixty, Juliette's mass of hair
is black as it has ever been;
she needs no brassière to uplift

and firm her marble breasts; her skin
is still unwrinkled, perfumed, quick
to welcome and provoke desire:
so, if you're bold enough to face
love's fiercest, most enduring fire,
call Juliette, and have no fears –
you'll soon forget those sixty years!

Ovid
43BC–AD17

'Your husband will be with us' (Elegy iv, Book I)

Your husband will be with us at the treat;
May that be the last supper he shall eat.
And am poor I, a guest invited there,
Only to see, while he may touch the fair?
To see you kiss and hug your nauseous lord,
While his lewd hand descends below the board?
Now wonder not that Hippodamia's[5] charms,
At such a sight, the centaurs urged to arms:
That in a rage, they threw their cups aside,
Assailed the bridegroom, and would force the bride.
I am not half a horse, (I wish I were):
Yet hardly can from you my hands forbear.
Take, then, my counsel; which, observed, may be
Of some importance both to you and me.
Be sure to come before your man be there,
There's nothing can be done, but come howe're.
Sit next him, (that belongs to decency);
But tread upon my foot in passing by.
Read in my looks what silently they speak,
And slyly, with your eyes, your answer make.
My lifted eyebrow shall declare my pain,
My right hand to his fellow shall complain:
And on the back a letter shall design;
Besides a note that shall be writ in wine.

When e're you think upon our last embrace,
With your forefinger gently touch your face.
If any word of mine offend my dear,
Pull, with your hand, the velvet of your ear.
If you are pleased with what I do or say,
Handle your rings, or with your fingers play.
As suppliants use at altars, use the board
When e're you wish the devil may take your lord.
When he fills for you, never touch the cup;
But bid th'officious cuckold drink it up.
The waiter on those services employ;
Drink you, and I will snatch it from the boy:
Watching the part where your sweet mouth has been,
And thence, with eager lips, will suck it in.
If he, with clownish manners thinks it fit
To taste, and offers you the nasty bit,
Reject his greasy kindness, and restore
Th'unsavoury morsel he had chewed before.
Nor let his arms embrace your neck, nor rest
Your tender cheek upon his hairy breast.
Let not his hand within your bosom stray,
And rudely with your pretty bubbies play.
But, above all, let him no kiss receive;
That's an offence I never can forgive.
Do not, O do not that sweet mouth resign,
Lest I rise up in arms; and cry 'tis mine.
I shall thrust in betwixt, and void of fear
The manifest adulterer will appear.
These things are plain to sight, but more I doubt
What you conceal beneath your petticoat.
Take not his leg between your tender thighs,
Nor, with your hand, provoke my foe to rise.
How many love-inventions I deplore,
Which I, myself, have practised all before!
How oft have I been forced the robe to lift
In company; to make a homely shift
For a bare bout, ill huddled o're in haste,
While o're my side the fair her mantle cast.

You to your husband shall not be so kind;
But, lest you should, your mantle leave behind.
Encourage him to tope, but kiss him not,
Nor mix one drop of water in his pot.
If he be fuddled well, and snores apace,
Then we may take advice from time and place.
When all depart, while compliments are loud,
Be sure to mix among the thickest crowd:
There I will be, and there we cannot miss,
Perhaps to grubble, or at least to kiss.
Alas, what length of labour I employ,
Just to secure a short and transient joy!
For night must part us; and when night is come,
Tucked underneath his arms he leads you home.
He locks you in, I follow to the door,
His fortune envy, and my own deplore.
He kisses you, he more than kisses too;
Th'outrageous cuckold thinks it all his due.
But, add not to his joy, by your consent;
And let it not be given, but only lent:
Return no kiss, nor move in any sort;
Make it a dull, and a malignant sport.
Had I my wish, he should no pleasure take,
But slubber o're your business for my sake.
And what e're fortune shall this night befall,
Coax me tomorrow, by foreswearing all.

'*In summer's heat*' (Elegy v, Book I)

In summer's heat, and mid-time of the day,
To rest my limbs upon a bed I lay;
One window shut, the other open stood,
Which gave such light as twinkles in a wood
Like twilight glimpse at setting of the sun,
Or night being past, and yet not day begun.
Such light to shamefast maidens must be shown,
Where they may sport and seem to be unknown.
Then came Corinna in a long loose gown,
Her white neck hid with tresses hanging down,

Resembling fair Semiramis[6] going to bed,
Or Lais of a thousand wooers sped.
I snatched her gown; being thin, the harm was small,
Yet strived she to be covered therewithall,
And striving thus as one that would be cast,
Betrayed herself, and yielded at the last.
Stark naked as she stood before mine eye,
Not one wen in her body could I spy.
What arms and shoulders did I touch and see,
How apt her breasts were to be pressed by me!
How smooth a belly under her waist saw I,
How large a leg, and what a lusty thigh!
To leave the rest, all liked me passing well;
I clinged her naked body, down she fell.
Judge you the rest: being tired she bade me kiss;
Jove send me more such afternoons as this.

'Graecinus (well I wot)' (Elegy x, Book II)

Graecinus (well I wot) thou told'st me once
I could not be in love with two at once.
By thee deceived, by thee surprised am I,
For now I love two women equally.
Both are well favoured, both rich in array,
Which is the loveliest it is hard to say.
This seems the fairest, so doth that to me,
And this doth please me most, and so doth she.
Even as a boat tossed by contrary wind,
So with this love and that, wavers my mind.
Venus, why doublest thou my endless smart?
Was not one wench enough to grieve my heart?
Why add'st thou stars to heaven, leaves to green woods,
And to the vast deep sea fresh water floods?
Yet this is better far than lie alone;
Let such as be mine enemies have none.
Yea, let my foes sleep in an empty bed,
And in the midst their bodies largely spread.
But may soft love rouse up my drowsy eyes,
And from my mistress' bosom let me rise.

Let one wench cloy me with sweet love's delight
If one can do't, if not, two every night.
Though I am slender, I have store of pith,
Nor want I strength, but weight, to press her with.
Pleasure adds fuel to my lustful fire,
I pay them home with that they most desire.
Oft have I spent the night in wantonness,
And in the morn been lively ne'er the less.
He's happy who love's mutual skirmish slays,
And to the gods for that death Ovid prays.
Let soldier chase his enemies amain,
And with his blood eternal honour gain;
Let merchants seek wealth and with perjured lips,
Being wracked, carouse the sea tired by their ships;
But when I die, would I might droop with doing,
And in the midst thereof, set my soil going,
That at my funerals some may weeping cry,
'Even as he led his life, so did he die.'

'Thou ring' (Elegy xv, Book II)

Thou ring that shalt my fair girl's finger bind,
Wherein is seen the giver's loving mind,
Be welcome to her, gladly let her take thee,
And her small joint's encircling round hoop make thee.
Fit her so well as she is fit for me,
And of just compass for her knuckles be.
Blest ring, thou in my mistress' hand shalt lie;
Myself, poor wretch, mine own gifts now envy.
O would that suddenly into my gift
I could myself by secret magic shift!
Then would I wish thee touch my mistress' pap,
And hide thy left hand underneath her lap;
I would get off though strait, and sticking fast,
And in her bosom strangely fall at last.
Then I, that I may seal her privy leaves,
Lest to the wax the hold-fast dry gem cleaves,
Would first my beauteous wench's moist lips touch,
Only I'll sign nought that may grieve me much.

I would not out, might I in one place hit,
But in less compass her small fingers knit.
My life, that I will shame thee never fear,
Or be a load thou shouldst refuse to bear.
Wear me, when warmest showers thy members wash,
And through the gem let thy lost waters pash.
But seeing thee, I think my thing will swell,
And even the ring perform a man's part well.
Vain things why wish I ? Go, small gift from hand,
Let her my faith with thee given understand.

'*Either she was foul*' (Elegy vii, Book III)

Either she was foul, or her attire was bad,
Or she was not the wench I wished t'have had.
Idly I lay with her, as if I loved not,
And like a burden grieved the bed that moved not.
Though both of us performed our true intent,
Yet could I not cast anchor where I meant.
She on my neck her ivory arms did throw,
Her arms far whiter than the Scythian snow,
And eagerly she kissed me with her tongue,
And under mine her wanton thigh she flung.
Yea, and she soothed me up, and called me 'Sir',
And used all speech that might provoke and stir.
Yet like as if cold hemlock I had drunk,
It mocked me, hung down the head, and sunk.
Like a dull cipher or rude block I lay,
Or shade or body was I, who can say?
What will my age do, age I cannot shun,
Seeing in my prime my force is spent and done?
I blush, that being youthful, hot and lusty,
I prove neither youth nor man, but old and rusty.
Pure rose she, like a nun to sacrifice,
Or one that with her tender brother lies.
Yet boarded I the golden Chie twice,
And Libas, and the white-cheeked Pitho thrice.
Corinna craved it in a summer's night,
And nine sweet bouts we had before daylight.

What, waste my limbs through some Thessalian charms?
May spells and drugs do silly souls such harms?
With virgin wax hath some imbased my joints,
And pierced my liver with sharp needle points?
Charms change corn to grass and make it die;
By charms are running springs and fountains dry.
By charms mast drops from oaks, from vines grapes fall,
And fruit from trees when there's no wind at all.
Why might not then my sinews be enchanted,
And I grow faint as with some spirit haunted?
To this add shame: shame to perform it quailed me,
And was the second cause why vigour failed me.
My idle thoughts delighted her no more
Than did the robe or garment which she wore.
Yet might her touch make youthful Pylius'[7] fire,
And Tithon[8] livelier than his years require.
Even her I had and she had me in vain,
What might I crave more, if I ask again?
I think the great gods grieved they had bestowed
The benefit which lewdly I forslowed.
I wished to be recieved in, in I get me;
To kiss, I kiss; to lie with her, she let me.
Why was I blest? Why made king to refuse it?
Chuff-like had I not gold and could not use it?
So in a spring thrives he that told so much,
And looks upon the fruits he cannot touch.
Hath any rose so from a fresh young maid
As she might straight have gone to church and prayed?
Well, I believe she kissed not as she should,
Nor used the sleight and cunning which she could.
Huge oaks, hard adamants might she have moved,
And with sweet words cause deaf rocks to have loved.
Worthy she was to move both gods and men,
But neither was I man nor lived then.
Can deaf ears take delight when Phemius[9] sings,
Or Thamyris[10] in curious-painted things?
What sweet thought is there but I had the same?
And one gave place still as another came.

Yet notwithstanding, like one dead it lay,
Drooping more than a rose pulled yesterday.
Now, when he should not jet, he bolts upright,
And craves his task, and seeks to be at fight.
Lie down with shame, and see thou stir no more,
Seeing now thou wouldst deceive me as before.
Thou cozen'st me: by thee surprised am I,
And bide sore loss with endless infamy.
Nay more, the wench did not disdain a whit
To take it in her hand and play with it,
But when she saw it would by no means stand,
But still drooped down, regarding not her hand,
'Why mock'st thou me', she cried, 'or being ill
Who bade thee lie down here against thy will?
Either th'art witched with blood of frogs new dead,
Or jaded cam'st thou from some other's bed.'
With that, her loose gown on, from me she cast her;
In skipping out her naked feet much graced her.
And lest her maid should know of this disgrace,
To cover it, spilt water in the place.

'*Seeing thou art fair*' (Elegy xiv, Book III)

Seeing thou art fair, I bar not thy false playing,
But let not me, poor soul, know of thy straying.
Nor do I give thee counsel to live chaste,
But that thou wouldst dissemble, when 'tis past.
She hath not trod awry that doth deny it;
Such as confess have lost their good names by it.
What madness is't to tell night pranks by day,
And hidden secrets openly to bewray?
The strumpet with the stranger will not do
Before the room be clear, and door put to.
Will you make shipwreck of your honest name,
And let the world be witness of the same?
Be more advised, walk as a puritan,
And I shall think you chaste, do what you can.
Slip still, only deny it when 'tis done,
And before folk immodest speeches shun.

The bed is for lascivious toyings meet;
There use all tricks, and tread shame under feet.
When you are up and dressed, be sage and grave,
And in the bed hide all the faults you have.
Be not ashamed to strip you, being there,
And mingle thighs, yours ever mine to bear.
There in your rosy lips my tongue entomb,
Practise a thousand sports when there you come.
Forbear no wanton words you there would speak,
And with your pastime let the bedstead creak.
But with your robes put on an honest face,
And blush, and seem as you were full of grace.
Deceive all; let me err, and think I am right,
And like a wittol think thee void of sleight.
Why see I lines so oft received and given,
This bed and that by tumbling made uneven,
Like one start up, your hair tossed and displaced,
And with a wanton's tooth your neck new-raced?
Grant this, that what you do I may not see;
If you weigh not ill speeches, yet weigh me.
My soul fleets when I think what you have done,
And thorough every vein doth cold blood run.
Then thee whom I must love I hate in vain,
And would be dead, but dead with thee remain.
I'll not sift much, but hold thee soon excused,
Say but thou wert injuriously accused.
Though while the deed be doing you be took,
And I see when you ope the two-leaved book,
Swear I was blind, deny, if you be wise,
And I will trust your words more than mine eyes.
From him that yields the palm is quickly got,
Teach but your tongue to say, 'I did it not',
And being justified by two words, think
The cause acquits you not, but I that wink.

'First then believe' (from *Ars Amatoria*, Book I)

First then believe, all women may be won;
Attempt with confidence, the work is done.
The grasshopper shall first forbear to sing,
In summer season, or the birds in spring;
Than women can resist your flattering skill:
Ev'n she will yield, who swears she never will.
To secret pleasure both the sexes move:
But women most, who most dissemble love.
'Twere best for us, if they would first declare;
Avow their passion, and submit to prayer.
The cow by lowing, tells the bull her flame:
The neighing mare invites her stallion to the game.
Man is more temperate in his lust than they;
And more than women, can his passion sway.

*   *   *

By letters, not by words, thy love begin,
And ford the dangerous passage with thy pen.
If to her heart thou aim'st to find the way,
Extremely flatter, and extremely pray.
Priam by prayers did Hector's body gain;
Nor is an angry god invoked in vain.
With promised gifts her easy mind bewitch;
For even the poor in promise may be rich.
Vain hopes a while her appetite will stay;
'Tis a deceitful, but commodious way.
Who gives is mad; but make her still believe
'Twill come, and that's the cheapest way to give.
Even barren lands fair promises afford;
But the lean harvest cheats the starving lord.
Buy not thy first enjoyment; lest it prove
Of bad example to thy future love:
But get it *gratis*; and she'll give thee more,
For fear of losing what she gave before.
The losing gamester shakes the box in vain,
And bleeds, and loses on, in hopes to gain.

*   *   *

Be not too finical; but yet be clean;
And wear well-fashioned clothes, like other men.
Let not your teeth be yellow, or be foul;
Nor in wide shoes your feet too loosely roul.
Of a black muzzle, and long beard beware;
And let a skilful barber cut your hair:
Your nails be picked from filth, and even pared;
Nor let your nasty nostrils bud with beard.
Cure your unsavoury breath; gargle your throat;
And free your armpits from the ram and goat.
Dress not, in short, too little, or too much:
And be not wholly French, nor wholly Dutch.

*   *   *

Act well the lover, let thy speech abound
In dying words, that represent thy wound.
Distrust not her belief; she will be moved:
All women think they merit to be loved.

*   *   *

Beg her, with tears, thy warm desires to grant;
For tears will pierce a heart of adamant.
If tears will not be squeezed, then rub your eye,
Or noint the lids, and seem at last to cry.
Kiss, if you can: resistance if she make,
And will not give you kisses, let her take.
Fie, fie, you naughty man, are words of course;
She struggles, but to be subdued by force.
Kiss only soft, I charge you, and beware,
With your hard bristles, not to brush the fair.
He who has gained a kiss, and gains no more,
Deserves to lose the bliss he got before.
If once she kiss, her meaning is expressed;
There wants but little pushing for the rest:
Which if thou dost not gain, by strength or art,
The name of clown then suits with thy desert.
'Tis downright dullness, and a shameful part.
Perhaps she calls it force; but if she 'scape,
She will not thank you for th'omitted rape.

The sex is cunning to conceal their fires,
They would be forced, even to their own desires.
They seem t'accuse you, with a downcast sight,
But in their souls confess you did them right.
Who might be forced, and yet untouched depart,
Thank with their tongues, but curse you with their heart.

*   *   *

    This is the sex; they will not first begin,
But when compelled, are pleased to suffer sin.
Is there, who thinks that women first should woo?
Lay by thy self-conceit, thou foolish beau.
Begin, and save their modesty the shame;
'Tis well for thee, if they receive thy flame.
'Tis decent for a man to speak his mind;
They but expect th'occasion to be kind.
Ask, that thou may'st enjoy; she waits for this:
And on thy first advance depends thy bliss.

Lucilius
1st century

'*Though Artist John*'

Though Artist John had twenty sons
he never got a likeness once.

Marcus Argentarius
1st century

'*Take those dark glasses off*'

Take those dark glasses off, Lucille,
They tease too much. And let your hips
roll less provocatively, for
the way that clinging satin slips

and slides on buttocks and on breasts
suggests the nakedness it hides
so clearly that you seem both stripped
and dressed at once. To be so eyed
by all the men may give you kicks,
but if you don't give up I swear
I'll take to clothes like that, half show,
Half hide a thing to make *you* stare.

'*In love with young Elaine*'

In love with young Elaine, at last
I talked her into it! We played
together, breathless, in my room;
our hearts were thumping, and, afraid
that someone might surprise our love,
we talked in whispers; but we had
been overheard – her Mother's face
poked round the bedroom door and said
'No cheating, now! Remember, Dear,
We share and share alike round here!'

Petronius
circa 20–66

'*Doing, a filthy pleasure is*'

Doing, a filthy pleasure is, and short;
And done, we straight repent us of the sport:
Let us not then rush blindly on unto it,
Like lustful beasts, that only know to do it:
For lust will languish, and that heat decay,
But thus, thus, keeping endless Holy-day,
Let us together closely lie, and kiss,
There is no labour, nor no shame in this;
This hath pleased, doth please, and long will please; never
Can this decay, but is beginning ever.

Martial

circa 40–circa 104

'*Wife, there are some points*' (Epigram 104, Book XI)

Wife, there are some points on which we differ from each other:
Either change your ways to mine or go back to your mother.
She, I grant, has brought you up to be a model daughter –
Bed at sunset, up at daybreak, drinking only water –
I, however, am no antique Roman, stiff and stern:
To me the night's for making love and drinking wine in turn.
You wear a nightgown, robe and girdle, even in hot weather:
I like sleeping with a woman in the altogether.
I want kisses long drawn out, lips parted, tongue-tips meeting:
Yours could just as well be your grandmother's morning greeting.
You think we should be in total darkness when we're screwing:
I prefer a light; I like to see what I am doing.
Women should cooperate, caressing, squirming, squealing:
You lie back and think of Rome, or contemplate the ceiling.
Hector's[11] house-slaves masturbated as, through half-shut doors,
They watched Andromache, astraddle, ride her hubby-horse.
That paragon of chastity, Penelope, would keep
Her hand there after Ulysses was snoring in his sleep.
You won't pretend to be a boy; such tricks, you say, don't suit us:
Julia lay prone for Pompey, Portia did for Brutus;
Even Jupiter, before he had his Ganymede,
Persuaded Juno to turn round to satisfy his need.
By all means be Lucrece and sit like Virtue on a dais
All day long, provided that in bed at night you're Lais.

Juvenal

circa 60–circa 130

'If then thy lawful spouse' (from Satire vi)

If then thy lawful spouse thou canst not love,
What reason should thy mind to marriage move?
Why all the charges of the nuptial feast,
Wines and desserts, and sweetmeats to digest;
Th'endowing gold that buys the dear delight;
Given for thy first and only happy night?
If thou art thus uxoriously inclined,
To bear thy bondage with a willing mind,
Prepare thy neck, and put it in the yoke:
But for no mercy from thy woman look.
For though, perhaps, she loves with equal fires,
To absolute dominion she aspires;
Joys in the spoils, and triumphs o'er thy purse;
The better husband makes the wife the worse.
Nothing is thine to give, or sell, or buy,
All offices of ancient friendship die;
Nor hast thou leave to make a legacy.
By thy imperious wife thou art bereft
A privilege, to pimps and panders left;
Thy testament's her will: where she prefers
Her ruffians, drudges and adulterers;
Adopting all thy rivals for thy heirs.

* * *

Thus the she-tyrant reigns, till pleased with change,
Her wild affections to new empires range:
Another subject-husband she desires;
Divorced from him, she to the first retires,
While the last wedding-feast is scarcely o're;
And garlands hang yet green upon the door.
So still the reckoning rises; and appears
In total sum, eight husbands in five years.
The title for a tombstone might be fit;
But that it would too commonly be writ.

Her mother living, hope no quiet day;
She sharpens her, instructs her how to flea
Her husband bare, and then divides the prey.
She takes love letters, with a crafty smile,
And, in her daughter's answer, mends the style.
In vain the husband sets his watchful spies;
She cheats their cunning, or she bribes their eyes.
The doctor's called; the daughter, taught the trick,
Pretends to faint; and in full health is sick.
The panting stallion at the closet door
Hears the consult, and wishes it were o're.
Can'st thou, in reason, hope, a bawd so known
Should teach her other manners than her own?
Her interest is in all th'advice she gives:
'Tis on the daughter's rents the mother lives.

*   *   *

Besides, what endless brawls by wives are bred:
The curtain-lecture makes a mournful bed.
Then, when she has thee sure within the sheets,
Her cry begins, and the whole day repeats.
Conscious of crimes herself, she teases first;
Thy servants are accused; thy whore is cursed;
She acts the jealous, and at will she cries:
For women's tears are but the sweat of eyes.
Poor cuckold-fool, thou think'st that love sincere,
And suck'st between her lips, the falling tear:
But search her cabinet and thou shalt find
Each tiller[12] there, with love epistles lined.
Suppose her taken in a close embrace,
This you would think so manifest a case,
No rhetoric could defend, no impudence outface:
And yet even then she cries the marriage vow,
A mental reservation must allow;
And there's a silent bargain still implied,
The parties should be pleased on either side:
And both may for their private needs provide.
'Though men yourselves, and women us you call,
Yet Homo is a common name for all.'

There's nothing bolder than a woman caught;
Guilt gives 'em courage to maintain their fault.

*   *   *

    What care our drunken dames to whom they spread?
Wine, no distinction makes of tail or head.
Who lewdly dancing at a midnight ball,
For hot eringoes,[13] and fat oysters call:
Full brimmers to their fuddled noses thrust;
Brimmers the last provocatives of lust.
When vapours to their swimming brains advance,
And double tapers on the tables dance.

    Now think what bawdy dialogues they have,
What Tullia talks to her confiding slave;
At modesty's old statue: when by night,
They make a stand, and from their litters light;
They straighten with their hands the nameless place
And spouting thence bepiss her venerable face:
Before the conscious moon they get astride;
By turns are ridden and by turns they ride.
The good man early to the levee goes,
And treads the nasty paddle of his spouse.

    The secrets of the goddess named the Good,
Are even by boys and barbers understood:
Where the rank matrons, dancing to the pipe,
Gig with their bums, and are for action ripe;
With music raised, they spread abroad their hair;
And toss their heads like an enamoured mare:
Confess their itching in their ardent eyes
While tears of wine run trickling down their thighs.
Laufella lays her garland by, and proves
The mimic lechery of manly loves,
Provokes to flats some battered household whore
And heaving up the rubster does adore.
Ranked with the lady, the cheap sinner lies;
For here not blood, but virtue gives the prize.
Nothing is feigned, in this venereal strife;
'Tis downright lust, and acted to the life.

So full, so fierce, so vigorous, and so strong;
That, looking on, would make old Nestor[14] young.
Impatient of delay, a general sound,
An universal groan of lust goes round;
For then, and only then, the sex sincere is found.
Now is the time for action; now begin,
They cry, and let the lusty lovers in.
The whoresons are asleep; then bring the slaves
And watermen, a race of strong-backed knaves:
Bring anything that's man: if none be nigh
Asses have better parts their places to supply.

* * *

I hear your cautious counsel, you would say,
Keep close your women, under lock and key:
But, who shall keep those keepers? Women, nursed
In craft, begin with those, and bribe 'em first.
The sex is all turned whore; they love the game;
And mistresses, and maids, are both the same.

Imr Al-Qais
6th century

from *Ode*

I twisted her side-tresses to me, and she leaned over me;
slender-waisted she was, and tenderly plump her ankles,
shapely and taut her belly, white-fleshed, not the least flabby,
polished the lie of her breast-bones, smooth as a burnished mirror.
She turns away, to show a soft cheek, and wards me off
with the glance of a wild deer of Wajra, a shy gazelle with its fawn;
she shows me a throat like the throat of an antelope, not ungainly
when she lifts it upwards, neither naked of ornament;
she shows me her thick black tresses, a dark embellishment
clustering down her back like bunches of a laden date-tree –
twisted upwards meanwhile are the locks that ring her brow,

she shows me a waist slender and slight as a camel's nose-rein,
and a smooth shank like the reed of a watered, bent papyrus.
In the morning the grains of musk hang over her couch,
sleeping the forenoon through, not girded and aproned to labour.

Paul the Silentiary
6th century

'Under her mother's nose'

Under her mother's nose
and avoiding her eye,
she slipped me a pair
of apples; as she pressed
them in my hands, Love rose
and made me curse
two apples in my grip
and not two breasts.

'Let's undress, Darling'

Let's undress, Darling, and lie nude,
each knotted in the other's arms;
let nothing come between us: that
last nylon wisp which veils your charms
to me seems more a wall of stone!
Away with it! Unveil! Unbind!
Come close and kiss! I'll say no more.
I hate loose talk of any kind.

Bhartrhari

died 651

'If the forest of her hair'[15]

If the forest of her hair
Calls you to explore the land,
And her breasts, those mountains fair,
Tempt that mountaineer, your hand—
   Stop! before it is too late:
   Love, the brigand, lies in wait.

'On sunny days'

On sunny days there in the shade
Beneath the trees reclined a maid
Who lifted up her dress (she said)
To keep the moonbeams off her head.

' "No! don't!" she says'

'No! don't!' she says at first, while she despises
The very thought of love; then she reveals
A small desire; and passion soon arises,
Shyly at first, but in the end she yields.
With confidence then playing without measure
Love's secret game, at last no more afraid
She spreads her legs wide in her boundless pleasure.
Ah! love is lovely with a lovely maid!

'Love goes a-fishing'

Love goes a-fishing with the rod Desire,
Baiting his hook with Woman for delight.
Attracted by the flesh, the men-fish bite.
He hauls them in and cooks them in his fire.

'In this vain world'

In this vain world, when men of intellect
Must soil their souls with service, to expect
A morsel at a worthless prince's gate,
How could they ever hope to renovate
Their spirits? – were it not that fate supplies
The swinging girdles and the lotus eyes –
Women, with swelling breasts that comfort soon,
Wearing the beauty of the rising moon.

'In this vain fleeting universe'

In this vain fleeting universe, a man
Of wisdom has two courses: first, he can
Direct his time to pray, to save his soul,
And wallow in religion's nectar-bowl;
But, if he cannot, it is surely best
To touch and hold a lovely woman's breast,
And to caress her warm round hips, and thighs,
And to possess that which between them lies.

Amaru

7th Century

'When his mouth'

When his mouth faced my mouth, I turned aside
And steadfastly gazed only at the ground;
I stopped my ears, when at each coaxing word
They tingled more; I used both hands to hide
My blushing, sweating cheeks. Indeed I tried.
But oh, what could I do, then, when I found
My bodice splitting of its own accord?

'Close in the tight embrace'

Close in the tight embrace her breasts were pressed,
Her skin thrilled; and between her pretty thighs
The oil-smooth sap of love has overflowed.
'No not again, my darling. Let me rest;
Don't make me . . .', whispering, pleading soft, she sighs.
Is she asleep? or dying? or else melted
Into my heart? Or is she but a dream?

'"Look darling . . ."'

'Look, darling, how we've disarranged the bed:
Now it's too hard with rubbed-off sandal-paste,
   Too rough for your soft skin,' he said,
   'Come, lie on me instead.'
While he distracted me with kisses sweet,
   All of a sudden, with his feet
   In pincer-fashion then he caught
   My sari firmly by the hem:
   And so the sly rogue forced me then
     To move the way he ought.

Walther von der Vogelweide
circa 1170–1230

'*Under the linden*'

Under the linden
Near the common
Where both of us had shared a bed;
There, lying where we'd lain,
You'll come upon
Some grass and flowers neatly spread.
Outside the forest in the dell
tarantara!
    sweetly sang the nightingale.

I came there only
To discover
My darling was already there;
That was when he called me
'Divine creature':
I'll always hold that greeting dear.
Some kisses! More than ten hundred!
tarantara!
    that's what made my lips so red.

I saw he'd made us
From the flowers
A beautifully luxuriant bed;
Some stranger who might pass
This bed of ours
Will smile, knowing why it was made.
The roses give the game away,
tarantara!
    they reveal where my head lay.

If anyone knew
He'd slept with me
(Which God forbid!) I'd die of shame;
What our bodies did and how
No one will know
Except, that is, for me and him

And of course the little bird,
tarantara!
  who's not going to say a word.

Lady Nijo
13th century

'*Ties of my undergowns*'

Ties of my undergowns undone,
The man uncared for –
Gossip soon will spread.

Francesco da Barberino
1264–1348

from *A Virgin Declares Her Beauties*

My bosom, which is very softly made,
Of a white even colour, without stain,
Bears two fair apples, fragrant, sweetly-savoured,
Gathered together from the tree of life
The which is in the midst of paradise.
And these no person ever yet has touched;
For out of nurse's and of mother's hands
I was, when God in secret gave them me.
These ere I yield I must know well to whom;
And for that I would not be robbed of them,
I speak not all the virtue that they have;
Yet thus far speaking: – blessed were the man
Who once should touch them, were it but a little; –
See them I say not, for that might not be.

Geoffrey Chaucer

1340–1400

from *The Wife of Bath's Prologue*

   I charged my spouse with infidelities
When he was so sick he could hardly rise.
This titillated him and he would dream
His wife beheld him with such high esteem.
My midnight walks were thus designed, I said,
To see the women that he took to bed.
That story covered up more than my mirth,
Such cunning is bequeathed to us at birth;
Spinning deceit and tears are gifts from God
And women live by them while menfolk nod.
There's one thing that I'm rather proud to say:
I've always managed to get my own way
By force or by pretence or grumbling
Or nagging, absolutely anything.
But bed, above all, was a battlefield
Where I, the victor, would refuse to yield.
I would vacate the bed immediately
I felt my husband's arm come over me
Until he paid a ransom for the prize
I kept a captive tight between my thighs.

* * *

   Then I would say, 'My darling have a peep
At Wilken, our timid little sheep;
Come here, husband, let me kiss your cheek.
You must learn how to be patient and meek,
And try to cultivate a clear conscience
Since you like to preach of Job's patience.
Practise what you preach, learn suffering;
Unless you do so, I'll teach you something,
How it is wise to keep your wife content.
One of us must lose the argument
And since men have reason that women lack
You lose each time – you must learn to hold back.

What's the matter, why do you groan and grunt?
Is all this fuss because you want my cunt?
Take it, go on then, you can have it all –
Saints preserve us! damn! but you love it well!
If I could put a price on my *belle chose*
And sell it, I'd walk as fresh as a rose.
But I will keep it for your own sweet tooth;
By God, you are to blame to tell the truth.'

from *Troilus and Criseyde*

Her slender arms, her soft and supple back,
Her tapered sides – all fleshly, smooth and white –
He stroked, and asked for favours at her neck,
Her snowish throat, her breasts so round and light;
Thus in this heaven he took his delight,
And smothered her with kisses upon kisses,
Till gradually he came to learn where bliss is.

Anonymous
15th century

Hey Nonny, I will love our Sir John and love any

O lord, so sweet Sir John doth kiss,
    At every time when he would play;
Of himself so pleasant he is,
    I have no power to say him nay.

Sir John loves me and I love him;
    The more I love him the more I may.
He says, 'sweetheart, come kiss me trim' –
    I have no power to say him nay.

Sir John to me is proffering
    For his pleasure right well to pay,
And in my box he puts his offering –
    I have no power to say him nay.

Sir John is taken in my mousetrap:
  Fain would I have him both night and day.
He gropeth so nicely about my lap,
  I have no power to say him nay.

Sir John giveth me relvis rings,   *glittering*
  With pretty pleasure for to assay –
Furs of the finest with other things:
  I have no power to say him nay.

François Villon
1431–85

The Old Woman Regretting the Time of her Youth

It seemed to me that I heard complain
A woman who was once a whore,
Wishing she were a girl again,
And in this manner speaking sore.
'Old age, you're proud, and a thief what's more!
Why have you swiftly laid me low?
Who would prevent me, if now I swore
To kill myself with a single blow?

'Old age has taken the powers away
That once my beauty ordained for me
Over clerks and churchmen and merchants gay.
There was never any man born, but he
Would have given his wealth to me happily,
(With some regret for what he would lose),
If I would have given him willingly
What even beggars today refuse.

'To many men I refused my love
(Little wisdom in this did I show),
For the love of a boy who was cunning enough,
On whom great gifts I did bestow.

I witheld from many, this I know –
By my soul, I loved the lad.
But he was rough and brought me woe;
He loved me but for the cash I had!

'And though he'd drawn me into wrong,
Trampling me so that love would go,
Though he dragged me like a faggot along,
When he asked a kiss, I loved him so
That I forgot my every woe!
Stained with evil, he greedily came
For kisses! How sleek did I then grow!
But what have I left of him? Sin and shame!

'He's been dead these thirty years and more,
And I am left grown old and grey.
When I think, alas! of the days of yore,
What I was, and what I've become today –
When, naked, I myself survey,
And see myself so greatly changed,
Poor, dry and thin, and wasted away –
Almost with anger am I enraged.

'Where's my forehead, that once was smooth,
My golden hair, brows arched and tall?
The pretty glance which, in my youth,
Held the cleverest men in thrall;
My straight nose, not too big or small,
My tiny ears – where are they gone?
My dimpled chin, my eyes' clear call,
And those fair lips of vermilion?

'Those slender shoulders, beautiful?
Long arms and hands both neat and nice?
Small nipples? Haunches, plump and full,
High built and of a proper size
To win, in amorous lists, the prize?
My loins so wide? That gracious spot
Set between firm and fleshy thighs,
Within its little garden plot?

'My hair is grey, my forehead wrinkled;
The eyebrows fallen; dimmed those eyes
Which once with laughter shone and twinkled,
And many rogues did once entice.
My hooked nose far from beauty lies;
My ears hang down, moss grows therein.
My face is dead, and the colour flies
From skinny lips and double chin.

'This is all human beauty's end –
Arms growing short, and hands constricting;
The shoulders crooked grown, and bend,
The nipples retreat and are shrivelling;
Like the breasts, the haunches are slackening;
The garden's foul! The thighs? Why these
Are no longer thighs, but are withering,
Speckled and blotched like sausages!

'We mourn the good times of long ago,
Poor mad old women, to one another,
Upon our haunches squatting low,
Like hanks of wool heaped up together.
A hemp that burns with sudden smother,
That swiftly flames and is swiftly out –
Once we were fair. But to each and other,
To men and women, this comes about!'

The Ballad of Villon and Fat Madge

What though the beauty I love and serve be cheap,
    Ought you to take me for a beast or fool?
All things a man could wish are in her keep;
    For her I turn swashbuckler in love's school.
    When folk drop in, I take my pot and stool
And fall to drinking with no more ado.
I fetch them bread, fruit, cheese, and water, too;
    I say all's right so long as I'm well paid;
'Look in again when your flesh troubles you,
    Inside this brothel where we drive our trade.'

But soon the devil's among us flesh and fell,
  When penniless to bed comes Madge my whore;
I loathe the very sight of her like hell.
  I snatch gown, girdle, surcoat, all she wore,
  And tell her, these shall stand against her score.
She grips her hips with both hands, cursing God,
Swearing by Jesus' body, bones, and blood,
  That they shall not. Then I, no whit dismayed,
Cross her cracked nose with some stray shiver of wood
  Inside this brothel where we drive our trade.

When all's made up she drops me a windy word,
  Bloats like a beetle puffed and poisonous:
Grins, thumps my pate, and calls me dickey-bird,
  And cuffs me with a fist that's ponderous.
  We sleep like logs, being drunken both of us;
Then when we wake her womb begins to stir;
To save her seed she gets me under her
  Wheezing and whining, flat as planks are laid:
And thus she spoils me for a whoremonger
  Inside this brothel where we drive our trade.

Blow, hail or freeze, I've bread here baked rent free!
Whoring's my trade, and my whore pleases me;
  Bad cat, bad rat; we're just the same if weighed.
We that love filth, filth follows us, you see;
Honour flies from us, as from her we flee
  Inside this brothel where we drive our trade.

John Skelton
1460–1529

from *The Manner of the World Nowadays*

So many cuckold-makers,
So many crakers,   *boasters*
And so many peace-brakers,
  Saw I never:

So much vain clothing
With cutting and jagging,
And so much bragging,
   Saw I never.

So many news and knacks,
So many naughty packs,
And so many that money lacks,
   Saw I never:
So many maidens with child
And wilfully beguiled,
And so many places untiled,
   Saw I never.

So many women blamed
And righteously defamed,
And so little ashamed,
   Saw I never:
Widows so soon wed
After their husbands be dead,
Having such haste to bed,
   Saw I never.

Pietro Aretino
1492–1557

'*Look here, look all of you*' (*Sonetti Lussuriosi 8*)

Look here, look all of you in love who doubt
At what love undertakes and makes you bear:
See how this fellow keeps his end up where
He fucks her as he carries her about.

And without going into all the schools
Of screwing at full length and by the book,
Learn how to do it well from him. And look:
When on the job you don't need words – just tools.

See how he's hung her on his arms; her knees
Are clinging to him high around each side:
He's clearly staggered at such joys as these.

Not worried by exhaustion, on they ride,
Equally pleased by all they do to please,
Dying to end in fucking suicide.

Straight to the point, nothing to hide,
They gasp there twined in pleasure, and intent:
As long as it goes on, they'll be content.

'Let's fuck, dear heart' (*Sonetti Lussuriosi 9*)

Let's fuck, dear heart, let's have it in and out,
For we're obliged to fuck for being born,
And as I crave for cunt, you ache for horn,
Because the world would not make sense without.

If after death it were decent to be had,
I'd say: Let's fuck, let's fuck so much we die;
There we'll all fuck – you, Adam, Eve, and I –
For they invented death and thought it bad.

Really it's true that if those first two thieves
Had never eaten that perfidious fruit,
We'd still know how to fuck (though not wear leaves).

But no more gossip now; let's aim and shoot
The prick right to the heart, and make the soul
Burst as it dies in concert with the root.

And could your generous hole
Take in as witnesses these bobbing buoys
For inside testimony of our joys?

'To do research' (*Sonetti Lussuriosi 11*)

'To do research on such a solemn cock,
Which turns over the lappets of my cunt,
I'd like to be transfigured all to quim –
And you to be converted all to prick.

'Because, if I was slot and you were knob,
I'd satisfy straight off my starving rut
And you'd draw like a pussy from my well
All that delights a plunging reel and rod.

'But since I can't be just the Human Hole
And you can't turn into the Total Tool,
Accept the kindly feelings of my twat.

'Then, pull the quick wit of my middle leg,
Short as it is – no snatching – drop your ring
Slowly, and I'll thrust up my bursting point.

   'And after, on my root
Let yourself go completely with your crotch,
For I'll be cock then, sure as you'll be cunt.'

Some More Cases of Love, With Solutions

I

Q: Brother Martin with Sister Charity one night
   Suddenly thought, when full-tilt up her belly,
   'We might breed Antichrist,' and pumped his jelly
   Into her arsehole. Was he wrong or right?

A: Lay-brother Martin's was a fine old stunt
   To come and not let Antichrist come too,
   By finishing up the arse the noble screw
   The half-baked sod had started off in front.

2

Q: A Jesuit was in the missionary
   Posture with Sister Lucy when his post,
   Being a stranger there itself, got lost.
   Well, was it sacrilege or sodomy?

A: Poor ignorant Jesuit, you could hardly call
   Him sacrilegious, but he was a dunce
   Not to know arse-sensations from a cunt's –
   Being a qualified sodomite, after all.

3

Q : Nun Marta in the darkness broke the po;
    The abbess screeched out: 'Fuck you for a prick!'
    And Marta got a cock inside her quick.
    Was this obedience sinful? Yes or no?

A : Nun Marta was religious and not dim
    To yield obedience with rare common sense
    To the abbess who set her penitence
    At putting someone's cock up in her quim.

4

Q : At the Jesuits' church, the sexton father's racked
    With lust; and keen to keep his lust in order
    He dips his balls and prick in holy water.
    Now is that sacrilege or a holy act?

A : The sexton father should be praised indeed
    If dipping balls and prick in holy water
    He kept his swingeing lechery in order,
    Staying free and easy from the sins of seed.

5

Q : The abbess woke up frantic after she
    Had dreamed all night of eating gooseberry fool,
    To find her mouth full of the abbot's tool.
    How had she sinned, though? Greed? Or lechery?

A : She didn't sin, as far as we make out,
    In either way. It was an accident –
    Although, if she had found it in her cunt
    Or up her arse, there might have been some doubt.

6

Q : Sister Prue, to relieve a bout of nerves
    Which blocked the flow of holy orisons,
    Had herself screwed by two fat friars at once.
    The question is, what penance she deserves.

A: If it was just to let her prayers out
   She had them penetrate her to the hilt,
   She needn't feel the smallest prick of guilt:
   There is no penance laid on the devout.

7
Q: Julia one day standing in some Gents'
   Took in her mouth her gigolo's cock, and quite
   Suddenly gave the thing a damn great bite.
   Was that the sin of greed, in any sense?

A: It wasn't a premeditated deed
   When Lady Julia took a bite of one
   Of her many gigolos' cocks, and not in fun –
   So it could hardly be the sin of greed.

8
Q: Unable to shit, and in despair, this chap
   Madly trying out anything to live,
   Had himself buggered for a laxative.
   Is it sinful not to die for a crap?

A: Since wilful death is certainly a sin,
   He did the right thing getting buggered first,
   Poor fellow: otherwise, he would have burst.
   Three cheers for carrying on through thick and thin!

9
Q: Wanting to know what love is, Livia had
   Someone over to screw her for a bit.
   A doubt arose, right in the midst of it:
   Could having a mere taste, like this, be bad?

A: No, tasting is no sin, one understands.
   But all the same, the sin she probes is lust:
   A girl who wants to try a cock out must
   Keep cool, or have a cock-up on her hands.

10

Q: Down from the balcony Sister Margaret's flanks
   Fell plump on Brother Charles's straining tarse,
   Which saved her life but quite broke up her arse.
   So should the Sister sue him, or say thanks?

A: Unless she'd dropped on Charles's crumpled horn,
   Making her bullseye ring his single dart,
   She would have died. So she must thank the part
   That gave her life for everything it's borne.

11

Q: A nun called Joan goes to the lavatory,
   Thinking it's free, and sits on Brother Dick,
   Threading her quim exactly with his prick.
   Has she broken her vows of chastity?

A: Because, not meaning sin or knowing how,
   Joan gave the hospitality of her guts
   To that proud prick, and maybe to those nuts,
   It's here declared she didn't break her vow.

12

Q: A man with a licence from the Pope to doff
   All sins whatever, on the spot, no bother,
   Throws a magnificent fuck at Reverend Mother,
   And then absolves her. Has he got her off?

A: Not just for having screwed her through and through,
   But even if he'd buggered her as well,
   With a licence that could extradite from Hell,
   If he absolved her, that was thorough too.

13

Q: Pitching and rolling wonderfully on Brother
   Biondo's chivalrous and hard-headed pole,
   The Sister bursts his bollocks and her hole.
   Should they lay a complaint against each other?

A: The amorous rapture's not just on one side,
   But interlocked and mutual, balls and bum
   Reciprocally bursting as they come.
   What? go to court? They'll let the matter slide.

14
Q: Brother Astolfo to reduce the tension
   Rubbed his prick on the arse of novices,
   And this asporged the floor with whitish fizz.
   Was this the sin Gomorrhans never mention?

A: Brother Astolfo is no Sodomite:
   He only rubbed it outside, round the edge;
   He never split their buttocks with his wedge.
   To punish him for that would not be right.

15
Q: Brother Albert, in the heat of the dog-days,
   Tossed off his novices to save their skins
   From idleness and its adjacent sins.
   Was this too worldly to deserve our praise?

A: Temptation always rules the idle will,
   So, good for him, if Albert tossed their midget
   Organs off; and if he'd fucked them rigid,
   That should be counted more heroic still.

16
Q: A wandering Franciscan had the luck,
   Screwing an abbess from behind, to lock
   Onto the wrong hole with his thoughtless cock.
   Now, has he sinned against nature in this fuck?

A: Backsliding is no sin, without intent:
   Fucking the abbess therefore the brown friar
   Did nothing unnatural, since he'd no desire
   To stick it up her fly-blown fundament.

Q: Having committed buggery on a Jew,
    Philip confesses, showing he's contrite.
    But absolution is refused outright.
    Does the sin rest with him? What should he do?

A: Bartolo turns on this deplorable sod
    (In chapter six), and the Derectals too,
    For not impaling him completely through,
    To avenge the crucifixion of our God.

Edmund Spenser
1552–99

from *The Faerie Queen*

(II. xii. 73)

And all that while, right over him she hung,
    With her false eyes fast fixed in his sight,
    As seeking medicine, whence she was stung,
    Or greedily depasturing delight:
    And oft inclining down with kisses light,
    For fear of waking him, his lips bedewed,
    And through his humid eyes did suck his sprite,
    Quite molten into lust and pleasure lewd;
Wherewith she sighed soft, as if his case she rued.

* * *

(II. xii. 77–80)

Upon a bed of roses she was laid,
    As faint through heat, or dight to pleasant sin,
    And was arrayed, or rather disarrayed,
    All in a veil of silk and silver thin,
    That hid no whit her alabaster skin,
    But rather showed more white, if more might be:
    More subtle web Arachne cannot spin,

Nor the fine nets, which oft we woven see
Of scorched dew, do not in th'air more lightly flee.

Her snowy breast was bare to ready spoil
  Of hungry eyes, which note therewith be filled,
  And yet through langour of her late sweet toil,
  Few drops, more clear than nectar, forth distilled,
  That like pure orient pearls adown it trilled,
  And her fair eyes sweet smiling in delight,
  Moistened their fiery beams, with which she thrilled
  Frail hearts, yet quenched not; like starry light
Which sparkling on the silent waves, does seem more bright.

The young man sleeping by her, seemed to be
  Some goodly swain of honourable place,
  That certes it great pity was to see
  Him his nobility so foul deface;
  A sweet regard, and amiable grace,
  Mixed with manly sterness did appear
  Yet sleeping, in his well proportioned face,
  And on his tender lips the downy hair
Did now but freshly spring, and silken blossoms bear.

His warlike arms, the idle instruments
  Of sleeping praise, were hung upon a tree,
  And his brave shield, full of old moniments,
  Was fowly razed, that none the signs might see;
  Ne for them, ne for honour cared he,
  Ne ought, that did to his advancement tend,
  But in lewd loves, and wasteful luxury,
  His days, his goods, his body he did spend:
O horrible enchantment, that him so did blend.

*   *   *

(III. xii. 45)

Lightly he clipped her twixt his arms twain,
  And straightly did embrace her body bright,
  Her body, late the prison of sad pain
  Now the sweet lodge of love and dear delight:
  But she fair lady overcomen quite

Of huge affection, did in pleasure melt,
And in sweet ravishment poured out her sprite:
No word they spake, nor earthly thing they felt,
But like two senseless stocks in long embracement dwelt.

'*Coming to kiss her lips*' (*Amoretti*, Sonnet 63)

Coming to kiss her lips, (such grace I found)
    Me seemed I smelt a garden of sweet flowers:
    That dainty odours from them threw around
    For damsels fit to deck their lovers' bowers.
Her lips did smell like unto gillyflowers,
    Her ruddy cheeks like unto roses red:
    Her snowy brows like budded bellamoures,
    Her lovely eyes like pinks but newly spread.
Her goodly bosom like a strawberry bed,
    Her neck like to a bunch of colombines:
    Her breast like lillies, ere their leaves be shed,
    Her nipples like young blossomed jessamines.
Such fragrant flowers do give most odorous smell,
    But her sweet odour did them all excell.

'*Fair bosom*' (*Amoretti*, Sonnet 76)

Fair bosom fraught with virtue's richest treasure,
    The nest of love, the lodging of delight:
    The bower of bliss, the paradise of pleasure,
    The sacred harbour of that heavenly sprite.
How was I ravished with your lovely sight,
    And my frail thoughts too rashly led astray?
    Whiles diving deep through amorous insight,
    On the sweet spoil of beauty they did pray.
And twixt her paps like early fruit in May,
    Whose harvest seemed to hasten now apace:
    They loosely did their wanton wings display,
    And there to rest themselves did boldly place.
Sweet thoughts I envy your so happy rest,
    Which oft I wished, yet never was so blessed.

'*Was it a dream*' (*Amoretti*, Sonnet 77)

Was it a dream, or did I see it plain,
    A goodly table of pure ivory:
    All spread with junkets, fit to entertain
    The greatest prince with pompous royalty.
'Mongst which there in a silver dish did lie
    Two golden apples of unvalued price:
    Far passing those which Hercules came by,
    Or those which Atlanta did entice.
Exceeding sweet, yet void of sinful vice,
    That many sought yet none could ever taste,
    Sweet fruit of pleasure brought from paradise
    By Love himself, and in his garden placed.
Her breast that table was so richly spread,
    My thoughts the guests, which would thereon have fed.

William Shakespeare
1564–1616

from *Venus and Adonis*

Who sees his true-love in her naked bed,
Teaching the sheets a whiter hue than white,
But when his glutton eye so full hath fed,
His other agents aim at like delight?
    Who is so faint that dares not be so bold,
    To touch the fire the weather being cold?

Ophelia's Song (from *Hamlet*)

By Gis, and by Saint Charity,
    Alack, and fie for shame!
Young men will do't, if they come to't;
    By cock, they are to blame.

Quoth she, 'before you tumbled me,
    You promised me to wed.'
'So would I ha' done, by yonder sun,
    An thou hadst not come to my bed.'

Thomas Nashe
1567–1601

The Choice of Valentines

It was the merry month of February
When young men in their jolly roguery
Rose early in the morn 'fore break of day
To seek them valentines so trim and gay.
With whom they may consort in summer sheen,
And dance the high degree on our town green.
As ales at easter or at pentecost
Perambulate the fields that flourish most,
And go to some village abordering near
To taste the cream, and cakes and such good cheer,
Or see a play of strange morality
Shown by bachelors of magnanimity;
Where to the country franklins flock-meal swarm,
And John and Joan come marching arm in arm,
Even on the hallows of that blessed saint,
That doeth true lovers with those joys acquaint,
I went poor pilgrim to my lady's shrine
To see if she would be my valentine.
But woe-alas, she was not to be found,
For she was shifted to an upper ground.
Good Justice Dudgeon with his crabbed face
With bills and staves had scared her from the place;
And now she was compelled for sanctuary
To fly unto a house of venery.
Thither went I, and boldly made enquire
If they had hackneys to let out to hire,

And what they craved by order of their trade
To let one ride a journey on a jade.
Therewith out stepped a foggy three-chinned dame,
That used to take young wenches for to tame,
And asked me, if I meant as I professed,
Or only asked a question but in jest.
'In jest?' quoth I; 'that term it as you will,
I come for game, therefore give me my Jill.'
'Why Sir,' quoth she, 'if that be your demand,
Come, lay me a God's penny in my hand;
For in our oratory sickerly,
None enters here to do his nicery.
But he must pay his offertory first,
And then perhaps we'll ease him of his thirst.'
I hearing her so earnest for the box
Gave her her due, and she the door unlocks.
In am I entered: Venus be my speed;
But where's this female, that must do this deed?
By blind meanders, and by crankled ways
She leads me onward (as my author says)
Until we came within a shady loft
Where Venus' bouncing vestals skirmish oft.
And there she set me in a leather chair,
And brought me forth of pretty trulls a pair,
To choose of them which might content mine eye;
But her I sought I could nowhere espy.
I spake them fair, and wished them well to fare,
Yet so it is, I must have fresher ware.
Wherefore, 'Dame Bawd, as dainty as you be,
Fetch gentle mistress Frances forth to me.'
'By Holy dame,' quoth she, 'and God's own mother,
I well perceive you are a wylie brother.
For, if there be a morsel of more price,
You'll smell it out, though I be ne'er so nice.
As you desire, so shall you swive with her,
But think your purse-strings shall a-buy it dear;
For, he that will eat quails must lavish crowns;
And mistress Frances in her velvet gowns,

And ruffs, and periwigs as fresh as May
Cannot be kept with half a crown a day.'
'Of price good hostess we will not debate,
Though you assize me at the highest rate;
Only conduct me to this bonny belle,
And ten good gobs I will unto thee tell
Of gold or silver, which shall like thee best,
So much do I her company request.'
Away she went: so sweet a thing is gold,
That (maugre) will invade the strongest hold.
Hey-ho, she comes, that hath my heart in keep,
Sing lullaby, my cares, and fall asleep.
Sweeping she comes, as she would brush the ground,
Her rattling silks my senses do confound.
Oh, I am ravished; void the chamber straight,
For, I must need's upon her with my weight.
'My Tomalin,' quoth she, and then she smiled,
'I, I,' quoth I; so more men are beguiled
With smiles, with flattering words, and feigned cheer,
When in their deeds their falsehood doeth appear.
'As how my lambkin?' (blushing, she replied)
'Because I in this dancing school abide?
If that be it, that breeds this discontent,
We will remove the camp incontinent.'
'For shelter only, sweetheart, came I hither,
And to avoid the troublous stormy weather.
But now the coast is clear, we will be gone,
Since but thyself, true lover I have none.'
With that she sprung full lightly to my lips,
And fast about the neck me colls and clips.
She wanton faints and falls upon her bed,
And often tosseth to and fro her head.
She shuts her eyes, and waggles with her tongue:
Oh, who is able to abstain so long?
I come, I come; sweet lady by thy leave,
Softly my fingers, up this curtain, heave
And make me happy stealing by degrees.
First bare her legs, then creep up to her knees.

From thence ascend unto her manly thigh
(A pox on lingering when I am so nigh).
Smock climb apace, that I may see my joys,
Oh heaven, and paradise are all but toys,
Compared with this sight, I now behold,
Which well might keep a man from being old.
A pretty rising womb without a weam,
That shone as bright as any silver stream;
And bare out like the bending of a hill,
At whose decline a fountain dwelleth still,
That hath his mouth beset with ugly briars
Resembling much a dusky net of wires.
A lofty buttock barred with azure veins,
Whose comely swelling, when my hand distrains,
It makes the fruits of love eftsoon be ripe;
And pleasure plucked too timely from the stem
To die ere it hath seen Jerusalem.
Oh Gods, that ever anything so sweet
So suddenly should fade away and fleet.
Her arms are spread, and I am all unarmed
Like one with Ovid's cursed hemlock charmed,
So are my limbs unwieldy for the fight,
That spend their strength in thought of her delight.
What shall I do to show myself a man?
It will not be for aught that beauty can.
I kiss, I clap, I feel, I view at will,
Yet dead he lies not thinking good or ill.
'Unhappy me,' quoth she, 'and wil't not stand?
Come, let me rub and chafe it with my hand.
Perhaps the silly worm is laboured sore,
And wearied that it can do no more.
If it be so (as I am great a-dread)
I wish ten thousand times, that I were dead.
How e'er it is; no means shall want in me,
That may avail to his recovery.'
Which said, she took and rolled it on her thigh,
And when she looked on't, she would weep and sigh,
And dandled it, and danced it up and down,
Not ceasing, till she raised it from his swoon.

And then he flew on her as he were wood,
And on her breech did thack, and foin a-good;
He rubbed, and pricked, and pierced her to the bones,
Digging as deep as he could dig for stones.
Now high, now low, now striking short and thick;
Now diving deep he touched her to the quick.
Now with a gird, he would his course rebate;
Straight would he take him to a stately gate,
Play while him list; and thrust he ne'er so hard,
Poor patient gristle lyeth at her ward,
And gives, and takes as blithe and free as May,
And e'ermore meets him in the middle way.
On him her eyes continually were fixed,
With her eye-beams his melting looks were mixed,
Which like the sun, that twixt two glasses plays
From one to th'other casts rebounding rays.
He like a star, that to regild his beams
Sucks in the influence of Phoebus' streams,
Imbathes the lines of his descending light
In the bright fountains of her clearest sight.
She fair as fairest planet in the sky
Her purity to no man doeth deny.
The very chamber, that enclouds her shine,
Looks like the palace of that God divine,
Who leads the day about the zodiac,
And every even descends to th'ocean lake:
So fierce and fervent is her radiance,
Such fiery stakes she darts at every glance,
As might enflame the icy limbs of age,
And make pale death his surquedry assuage
To stand and gaze upon her orient lamps
Where Cupid all his chiefest joys encamps,
And sits, and plays with every atomy
That in her sunbeams swarm abundantly.
Thus gazing, and thus striving we persevere,
But what so firm, that may continue ever?
'Oh not so fast,' my ravished mistress cries,
'Lest my content, that on thy life relies

Be brought too soon from his delightful seat,
And me unawares of hoped bliss defeat.
Together let our equal motions stir,
Together let us live and die my dear,
Together let us march unto content,
And be consumed with one blandishment.'
As she prescribed, so kept we crotchet-time,
And every stroke in order like a chime.
Whilst she, that had preserved me by her pity,
Unto our music framed a groaning ditty.
Alas, alas, that love should be a sin,
Even now my bliss and sorrow doeth begin.
Hold wide thy lap, my lovely Danae,
And entertain the golden shower so free,
That trilling falls into thy treasury,
As April drops not half so pleasant be,
Nor Nilus overflow, to Egypt plains,
As this sweet stream, that all her joints embaynes;
With *Oh*, and *Oh*, she itching moves her hips,
And to and fro, full lightly starts and skips.
She jerks her legs, and sprawleth with her heels,
No tongue may tell the solace that she feels.
I faint, I yield; Oh death rock me asleep;
Sleep – sleep desire, entombed in the deep.
'Not so my dear,' my dearest saint replied;
'For, from us yet thy spirit may not glide
Until the sinewy channels of our blood
Withold their source from this imprisoned flood;
And then will we (that then will come too soon)
Dissolved lie as though our days were done.
The whilst I speak, my soul is fleeting hence,
And life forsakes his fleshy residence.
Stay, stay sweet joy, and leave me not forlorn,
Why shouldst thou fade, that art but newly born?
Stay but an hour; an hour is not so much,
But half an hour; if that thy haste be such:
Nay but a quarter; I will ask no more,
That thy departure (which torments me sore)

May be alightened with a little pause,
And take away this passion's sudden cause.
He hears me not, hard-hearted as he is:
He is the son of Time, and hates my bliss.
Time ne'er looks back, the rivers ne'er return;
A second spring must help me or I burn.'
'No, no, the well is dry that should refresh me,
The glass is run of all my destiny.
Nature of winter learneth nigardise,
Who, as he overbears the stream with ice,
That man nor beast may of their pleasance taste,
So shuts she up her conduit all in haste,
And will not let her nectar overflow,
Lest mortal men immortal joys should know.'
'Adieu unconstant love, to thy disport,
Adieu false mirth, and melody too-short.
Adieu faint-hearted instrument of lust,
That falsely hast betrayed our equal trust.
Henceforth no more will I implore thine aid,
Or thee, or men of cowardice upbraid.
My little dildo shall supply their kind:
A knave, that moves as light as leaves by wind;
That bendeth not, nor foldeth any deal,
But stands as stiff, as he were made of steel,
And plays at peacock twixt my legs right blithe,
And doeth my tickling assuage with many a sigh;
For, by Saint Runnion he'll refresh me well,
And never make my tender belly swell.'
Poor Priapus, whose triumph now must fall,
Except thou thrust this weakling to the wall.
Behold how he usurps in bed and bower,
And undermines thy kingdom every hour.
How sly he creeps betwixt the bark and tree,
And sucks the sap, whilst sleep detaineth thee.
He is my mistress' page at every sound,
And soon will tent a deep entrenched wound.
He waits on courtly nymphs, that be so coy,
And bids them scorn the blind-alluring boy.

He gives young girls their gamesome sustenance,
And every gaping mouth his full sufficience.
He fortifies disdain with foreign arts,
And wanton-chaste deludes all loving hearts.
If any wight a cruel mistress serves,
Or in despair (unhappy) pines and starves
Curse eunuch dildo, senseless, counterfeit,
Who sooth may fill, but never can beget:
But if revenge enraged with despair,
That such a dwarf his welfare should impair,
Would fain this woman's secretary know,
Let him attend the marks that I shall show.
He is a youth almost two handfulls high,
Straight, round, and plumb, yet having but one eye,
Wherein the rheum so fervently doeth reign,
That Stygian gulf may scarce his tears contain;
Attired in white velvet or in silk,
And nourished with hot water or with milk;
Armed otherwise in thick congealed glass,
When he more glib to hell below would pass,
Upon a charriot of five wheels he rides,
The which an arm-strong driver steadfast guides,
And often alters pace, as ways grow deep;
(For, who in paths unknown, one gate can keep?)
Sometimes he smoothly slideth down the hill;
Another while the stones his feet do kill:
In clammy ways he treadeth by and by,
And plasheth and sprayeth all that be him nigh.
So fares this jolly rider in his race,
Plunging, and sourcing forward in like case,
Bedashed, bespurted, and beplodded foul,
God give thee shame, thou blind mishapen owl.
Fy, fy for grief; a lady's chamberlain,
And canst not thou thy tattling tongue refrain?
I rede thee beardless blab, beware of stripes,
And be advised what thou vainly pipes.
Thou wilt be whipped with nettles for this gear
If Cicely show but of thy knavery here.

Saint Denis shield me from such female sprites.
Regard not Dames, what Cupid's poet writes.
I penned this story only for myself,
Who giving suck unto a childish elf,
And quite discouraged in my nursery,
Since all my store seems to her, penury.
I am not as was Hercules the stout,
That to the seventh journey could hold out.
I want those herbs and roots of Indian soil,
That strengthen weary members in their toil;
Drugs and electuaries of new device
Do shun my purse; that trembles at the price.
Sufficeth, all I have, I yield her hole,
Which for a poor man is a princely dole.
I pay our hostess scot and lot at most,
And look as lean and lank as any ghost.
What can be added more to my renown?
She lyeth breathless, I am taken down,
The waves do swell, the tides climb o'er the banks,
Judge gentlemen if I deserve not thanks,
And so goodnight unto you every one,
For lo, our thread is spun, our play is done.

Barnabe Barnes
1569–1609

'Soft, lovely, rose-like lips'

Soft, lovely, rose-like lips, conjoined with mine,
    Breathing out precious incense such,
(Such as, at Paphos, smokes to Venus' shrine)
    Making my lips immortal with their touch,
My cheeks, with touch of thy soft cheeks divine,
    Thy soft warm cheeks which Venus favours much;

Those arms, such arms, which me embraced,
    Me with immortal cincture girding round,
    Of everlasting bliss, then bound
With her enfolded thighs in mine entangled,
And both in one self-soul placed,
    Made a hermaphrodite with pleasure ravished.
There heat for heat's, soul for soul's empire wrangled;
    Why died not I with love so largely lavished?
For waked (not finding truth of dreams before)
It secret vexeth ten times more.

Giambattista Marino
1569–1625

Woman Washing Her Legs

Over a silver base, in a gold shell
I saw two alabaster columns stride
Against the perfumed and crystalline tide
Breaking up heaps of pearls in the white swell.

O resting-place where sorrow comes for ease
(I said), O end of nature and of love,
Pale boundary-marks set up by one above
In the sweet ocean of their ecstasies –

If only I were Hercules! I could
Transplant you in my arms and erect new
Trophies where man's desire has never stood;

Or else, like Samson, clasp and tumble you,
Burying death in your delicious fall,
With sorrow dying happily first of all.

John Donne
1572–1631

Love's Progress (Elegy xviii)

Who ever loves, if he do not propose
The right true end of love, he's one that goes
To sea for nothing but to make him sick:
Love is a bear-whelp born, if we o're lick
Our love, and force it new strange shapes to take,
We err, and of a lump a monster make.
Were not a calf a monster that were grown
Faced like a man, though better than his own?
Perfection is in unity: prefer
One woman first, and then one thing in her.
I, when I value gold, may think upon
The ductliness, the application,
The wholesomeness, the ingenuity,
From rust, from soil, from fire ever free:
But if I love it, 'tis because 'tis made
By our new nature (Use) the soul of trade.
  All these in women we might think upon
(If women had them) and yet love but one.
Can men more injure women than to say
They love them for that, by which they're not they?
Makes virtue woman? must I cool my blood
Till I both be, and find one wise and good?
May barren angels love so. But if we
Make love to woman; virtue is not she:
As beauty's not nor wealth: he that strays thus
From her to hers, is more adulterous,
Than if he took her maid. Search every sphere
And firmament, our Cupid is not there:
He's an infernal god and underground,
With Pluto dwells, where gold and fire abound:
Men to such gods, their sacrificing coles
Did not in altars lay, but pits and holes.
Although we see celestial bodies move
Above the earth, the earth we till and love:

So we her airs contemplate, words and heart,
And virtues; but we love the centric part.

   Nor is the soul more worthy, or more fit
For love, than this, as infinite as it.
But in attaining this desired place
How much they err; that set out at the face?
The hair a forest is of ambushes,
Of springs, snares, fetters and manacles:
The brow becalms us when 'tis smooth and plain,
And when 'tis wrinkled, shipwrecks us again.
Smooth, 'tis a paradise, where we would have
Immortal stay, and wrinkled 'tis our grave.
The nose (like to the first meridian) runs
Not 'twixt an east and west, but 'twixt two suns;
It leaves a cheek, a rosy hemisphere
On either side, and then directs us where
Upon the islands fortunate we fall,
(Not faint Canaries, but Ambrosial)
Her swelling lips; to which when we are come,
We anchor there, and think ourselves at home,
For they seem all: there sirens' songs, and there
Wise Delphic oracles do fill the ear;
There in a creek where chosen pearls do swell,
The remora,[16] her cleaving tongue doth dwell.
These, and the glorious promontory, her chin
Oar past; and the straight Hellespont between
The Sestos and Abydos[17] of her breasts,
(Not of two lovers, but two loves the nests)
Succeeds a boundless sea, but yet thine eye
Some island moles may scattered there descry;
And sailing towards her India, in that way
Shall at her fair Atlantic navel stay;
Though thence the current be thy pilot made,
Yet ere thou be where thou wouldst be embayed,
Thou shalt upon another forest set,
Where many shipwreck, and no further get.
When thou art there, consider what this chase
Mispent by thy beginning at the face.

    Rather set out below; practise my art,
Some symmetry the foot hath with that part
Why thou dost seek, and is thy map for that
Lovely enough to stop, but not stay at:
Least subject to disguise and change it is;
Men say the devil never can change his.
It is the emblem that hath figured
Firmness; 'tis the first part that comes to bed.
Civility we see refined: the kiss
Which at the face began, transplanted is,
Since to the hand, since to the imperial knee,
Now at the papal foot delights to be:
If kings think that the nearer way, and do
Rise from the foot, lovers may do so too;
For as free spheres move faster far than can
Birds, whom the air resists, so may that man
Which goes this empty and ethereal way,
Than if at beauties' elements he stay.
Rich nature hath in women wisely made
Two purses, and their mouths aversely laid:
They then, which to the lower tribute owe,
That way which that exchequer looks, must go:
He which doth not, his error is as great,
As who by clyster[18] gave the stomach meat.

To His Mistress Going to Bed (Elegy xix)

Come, Madam, come, all rest my powers defy,
Until I labour, I in labour lie.
The foe oft-times having the foe in sight,
Is tired with standing though he never fight.
Off with that girdle, like heaven's zone glistering,
But a far fairer world encompassing.
Unpin that spangled breastplate which you wear,
That th'eyes of busy fools may be stopped there.
Unlace yourself, for that harmonious chime,
Tells me from you, that now it is bedtime.
Off with that happy busk, which I envy,
That still can be, and still can stand so nigh.

Your gown going off, such beauteous state reveals,
As when from flowery meads th'hills shadow steals.
Off with that wiry coronet and show
The hairy diadem which on you doth grow:
Now off with those shoes, and then safely tread
In this love's hallowed temple, this soft bed.
In such white robes, heaven's angels used to be
Received by men; thou angel bring'st with thee
A heaven like Mahomet's paradise; and though
Ill spirits walk in white, we easily know,
By this these angels from an evil sprite,
Those set our hairs, but these our flesh upright.

 License my roving hands, and let them go,
Before, behind, between, above, below.
O my America! my new-found-land,
My kingdom, safeliest when with one man manned,
My mine of precious stones, my empery,
How blest am I in this discovering thee,
To enter in these bonds, is to be free;
Then there where my hand is set, my seal shall be.

 Full nakedness! All joys are due to thee,
As souls unbodied, bodies unclothed must be,
To taste whole joys. Gems which you women use
Are like Atlanta's balls, cast in men's views,
That when a fool's eye lighteth on a gem,
His earthly soul may covet their's, not them.
Like pictures, or like books' gay coverings made
For laymen, are all women thus arrayed;
Themselves are mystic books, which only we
(Whom their imputed grace will dignify)
Must see revealed. Then since that I may know;
As liberally, as to a midwife, show
Thyself: cast all, yea, this white linen hence,
Here is no penance, much less innocence.

 To teach thee, I am naked first; why then
What need'st thou have more covering than a man?

William Drummond of Hawthorden

1585–1649

from '*It was the time when to our Northern Pole*' (Song I)

Her lips like rows of coral soft did swell,
And th'one like th'other only doth excell:
The Tyrian fish looks pale, pale look the roses,
The rubies pale, when mouth's sweet cherry closes.
Her chin like silver Phoebe did appear
Dark in the midst to make the rest more clear:
Her neck seemed framed by curious Phidias' master,
Most smooth, most white, a piece of alabaster.
Two foaming billows flowed upon her breast,
Which did their tops with coral red encrest:
There all about as brooks them sport at leisure,
With circling branches veins did swell in azure:
Within those crooks are only found those isles
Which 'fortunate' the dreaming old world styles.
The rest the streams did hide, but as a lilly
Sunk in a crystal's fair transparent belly.

Robert Herrick

1591–1674

No Bashfulness in Begging

To get thine ends, lay bashfulness aside;
Who fears to ask, doth teach to be denied.

Upon Julia's Fall

Julia was careless, and withall,
She rather took, then got a fall:
The wanton ambler chanced to see
Part of her leg's sincerity:

And ravished thus, it came to pass,
The nag (like to the Prophet's ass)
Began to speak, and would have been
A telling what rare sights h'ad seen:
And had told all; but did refrain,
Because his tongue was tied again.

The Shoe Tying

Anthea bade me tie her shoe;
I did; and kissed the instep too:
And would have kissed unto her knee,
Had not her blush rebuked me.

The Vine

I dreamed this mortal part of mine
Was metamorphosed to a vine;
Which crawling one and every way,
Enthralled my dainty Lucia.
Me thought, her long small legs and thighs
I with my tendrils did surprise;
Her belly, buttocks, and her waist
By my soft nervelets were embraced:
About her head I writhing hung,
And with rich clusters (hid among
The leaves) her temples I behung
So that my Lucia seemed to me
Young Bacchus ravished by his tree.
My curls about her neck did crawl,
And arms and hands they did enthrall:
So that she could not freely stir,
(All parts there made one prisoner.)
But when I crept with leaves to hide
Those parts, which maids keep unespied,
Such fleeting pleasures there I took,
That with the fancy I awoke;
And found (Ah me!) this flesh of mine
More like a stock, than like a vine.

To Anthea

Ah my Anthea! must my heart still break?
(*Love makes me write, what shame forbids to speak.*)
Give me a kiss, and to that kiss a score;
Then to that twenty, add an hundred more:
A thousand to that hundred: so kiss on,
To make that thousand up a million.
Treble that million, and when that is done,
Let's kiss afresh, as when we first begun.
But yet, though love likes well such scenes as these,
There is an act that will more fully please:
Kissing and glancing, soothing, all make way
But to the acting of this private play:
Name it I would; but being blushing red,
The rest I'll speak, when we meet both in bed.

The Bag of the Bee

About the sweet bag of a bee,
    Two Cupids fell at odds;
And whose the pretty prize should be,
    They vowed to ask the Gods.

Which Venus hearing; thither came,
    And for their boldness stripped them:
And taking thence from each his flame;
    With rods of myrtle whipped them.

Which done, to still their wanton cries,
    When quiet grown sh'ad seen them,
She kissed, and wiped their dove-like eyes;
    And gave the bag between them.

The Definition of Beauty

Beauty, no other thing is, than a beam
Flashed out between the middle and extreme.

Upon Scobble

Scobble for whoredom whips his wife; and cries,
He'll slit her nose; but blubbering, she replies,
'Good sir, make no more cuts i'th'outward skin,
One slit's enough to let adultery in.'

The Vision

Sitting alone (as one forsook)
Close by a silver-shedding brook;
With hands held up to love, I wept;
And after sorrows spent, I slept:
Then in a vision I did see
A glorious form appear to me:
A virgin's face she had; her dress
Was like a sprightly Spartaness.
A silver bow with green silk strung,
Down from her comely shoulders hung:
And as she stood, the wanton air
Dandled the ringlets of her hair.
Her legs were such Diana shows,
When tucked up she a hunting goes;
With buskins shortened to descry
The happy dawning of her thigh:
Which when I saw, I made access
To kiss that tempting nakedness:
But she forbad me, with a wand
Or myrtle she had in her hand:
And chiding me, said, 'Hence, remove,
Herrick, thou art too coarse to love.'

Julia's Petticoat

Thy azure robe, I did behold,
As airy as the leaves of gold;
Which erring here, and wandering there,
Pleased with transgressions everywhere:

Sometimes 'twould pant, and sigh, and heave,
As if to stir it scarce had leave:
But having got it; thereupon,
'Twould make a brave expansion.
And pounced with stars, it showed to me
Like a celestial canopy.
Sometimes 'twould blaze, and then abate,
Like to a flame grown moderate:
Sometimes away 'twould wildly fling;
Then to thy thighs so closely cling,
That some conceit did melt me down,
As lovers fall into a swoon:
And all confused, I there did lie
Drowned in delights; but could not die.
That leading cloud, I followed still,
Hoping t'have seen of it my fill;
But ah! I could not: should it move
To life eternal, I could love.

Upon Julia's Breasts

Display thy breasts, my Julia, there let me
Behold that circummortal purity:
Between those glories, there my lips I'll lay,
Ravished, in that fair *Via Lactea*.

Her Bed

See's thou that cloud as silver clear,
Plump, soft, and swelling everywhere?
Tis Julia's bed, and she sleeps there.

Her Leg

Fain would I kiss my Julia's dainty leg,
Which is as white and hairless as an egg.

Clothes Do But Cheat and Cozen Us

Away with silks, away with lawn,
I'll have no scenes, or curtains drawn:
Give me my mistress, as she is,
Dressed in her nak'd simplicities:
For as my heart, e'en so mine eye
Is won with flesh, not drapery.

To Dianeme

Show me thy feet; show me thy legs, thy thighs;
Show me those fleshy principalities;
Show me that hill (where smiling love doth sit)
Having a living fountain under it.
Show me thy waist; then let me there withal,
By the ascension of thy lawn, see all.

Upon the Nipples of Julia's Breast

Have you beheld (with much delight)
A red rose peeping through a white?
Or else a cherry (double graced)
Within a lilly? Centre placed?
Or ever marked the pretty beam,
A strawberry shows half drowned in cream?
Or seen rich rubies blushing through
A pure smooth pearl, and orient too?
So like to this, nay all the rest,
Is each neat niplet of her breast.

Fresh Cheese and Cream

Would you have fresh cheese and cream?
Julia's breast can give you them:
And if more; each nipple cries,
To your cream, here's strawberries.

A Kiss

What is a kiss? Why this, as some approve;
The sure sweet-cement, glue, and lime of love.

Upon Julia's Clothes

When as in silks my Julia goes,
Then, then (methinks) how sweetly flows
That liquefaction of her clothes.

Next, when I cast mine eyes and see
That brave vibration each way free;
O how that glittering taketh me!

Kisses Loathsome

I abhor the slimy kiss,
(Which to me most loathsome is.)
Those lips please me which are placed
Close, but not too strictly laced:
Yielding I would have them; yet
Not a wimbling tongue admit:
What would poking-sticks make there,
When the ruff is set elsewhere?

Upon Julia's Washing Herself in the River

How fierce was I, when I did see
My Julia wash herself in thee!
So lillies through crystal look:
So purest pebbles in the brook:
As in the river Julia did,
Half with a lawn of water hid,
Into thy streams myself I threw,
And struggling there, I kissed thee too;
And more had done (it is confessed)
Had not thy waves forbad the rest.

The Description of a Woman

Whose head befringed with bescattered tresses
Seems like Apollo's when the morn he blesses
Or like unto Aurora when she sets
Her long dishevelled rose-crowned tramalets.
Her forehead smooth full polished bright and high
Bares in itself a graceful majesty
Under the which two crawling eyebrows twine
Like to the tendrils of a flattering vine
Under whose shades two starry sparkling eyes
Are beautified with fair fringed canopies.
Her comely nose with uniformal grace
Like purest white stands in the middle place
Parting the pair as we may well suppose
Each cheek resembling still a damask rose
Which like a garden manifestly show
How roses, lillies and carnations grow
Which sweetly mixed both with white and red
Like rose leaves, white and red seem mingled.
There nature for a sweet allurement sets
Two smelling swelling bashful cherrilets
The which with ruby redness being tipped
Do speak a virgin merry cherry-lipped
Over the which a meet sweet skin is drawn
Which makes them show like roses under lawn.
These be the ruby portals and divine
Which ope themselves to show an holy shrine
Whose breath is rich perfume, that to the sense
Smells like the burned Sabian frankincense
In which the tongue, though but a member small,
Stands guarded with a rosy hilly wall
And her white teeth which in the gums are set
Like pearl and gold make one rich carcanet.
Next doth her chin with dimpled beauty strive
For his plump white and smooth prerogative
At whose fair top to please the sight there grows
The blessed image of a blushing rose

Moved by the chin whose motion causeth this
That both her lips do part, do meet, do kiss.
Her ears which like two labyrinths are placed
On either side with rich rare jewells graced
Moving a question whether that by them
The gem is graced or they graced by the gem?
But the foundation of this architect
Is the swan-staining fair rare stately neck
Which with ambitious humbleness stands under
Bearing aloft this rich round world of wonder
In which the veins implanted seem to lie
Like loving vines hid under ivory
So full of claret that who so pricks a vine
May see it sprout forth streams of muscadine.
Her breast (a place for beauty's throne most fit)
Bears up two globes where love and pleasure sit
Which headed with two rich round rubies show
Like wanton rose buds growing out of snow;
And in the milky valley that's between
Sits Cupid kissing of his mother Queen
Fingering the paps that feel like sleeded silk
And pressed a little they will weep new milk.
Then comes the belly seated next below
Like a fair mountain of Riphean snow
Where nature in a whiteness without spot
Hath in the middle tied a Gordian knot;
Or else that she on that white waxen hill
Hath sealed the promise of her utmost skill.
But now my muse hath spied a dark descent
For this so peerless precious prominent,
A milky high way that direction yields
Unto the port mouth of th'Elysian fields:
A place desired of all but got by these
Whom love admits to this Hesperides.
Here's golden fruit that far exceeds all price
Growing in this love-guarded paradise,
Above the entrance there is written this:
'This is the portal to the bower of bliss'

(Through midst thereof a crystal stream there flows
Passing the sweet sweet of a musky rose).
Now love invites me to survey her thighs
Swelling in likeness like two crystal skies
With plump soft flesh of mettle pure and fine
Resembling shields both smooth and crystalline:
Hence rise those two ambitious hills that look
Into the middle most sight-pleasing crook
Which, for the better beautifying, shrouds
Its humble self twixt two aspiring clouds
Which to the knees by nature fastened on
Derive their ever well graced motion.
Her legs with two clear calves like silver tried
Kindly swell up with little pretty pride
Leaving a distance for the beauteous small
To beautify the leg and foot withall.
Then lowly yet most lovely stand the feet
Round, short and clear, like pounded spices sweet;
And whatsoever thing they tread upon
They make it scent like bruised cinnamon.
The lovely shoulders now allure the eye
To see two tablets of pure ivory
From which two arms like branches seem to spread
With tender rine and silver coloured,
With little hands and fingers long and small
To grace a lute, a viol, virginal.
In length each finger doth his next excel,
Each richly headed with a pearly shell
Richer than that fair precious virtuous horn
That arms the forehead of the unicorn.
Thus every part in contrariety
Meets in the whole and makes a harmony
As divers strings do singly disagree
But formed by number make sweet melody.
Unto the idol of the work divine
I consecrate this loving work of mine
Bowing my lips unto that stately root
Whence beauty springs, and thus I kiss thy foot.

Thomas Carew

1595–1640

Boldness in Love

Mark how the bashful morn, in vain
Courts the amorous marigold,
With sighing blasts, and weeping rain;
Yet she refuses to unfold.
But when the planet of the day,
Approacheth with his powerful ray,
Then she spreads, then she receives
His warmer beams into her virgin leaves.
So shalt thou thrive in love, fond boy;
If thy tears, and sighs discover
Thy grief, thou never shalt enjoy
The just reward of a bold lover:
But when with moving accents, thou
Shalt constant faith, and service vow,
Thy Celia shall receive those charms
With open ears, and with unfolded arms.

The Compliment

O my dearest I shall grieve thee
When I swear, yet sweet believe me,
By thine eyes the tempting book
On which even crabbed old men look
I swear to thee, (though none abhor them)
Yet I do not love thee for them.

I do not love thee for that fair,
Rich fan of thy most curious hair;
Though the wires thereof be drawn
Finer than the threads of lawn,
And are softer than the leaves
On which the subtle spinner weaves.

I do not love thee for those flowers,
Growing on thy cheeks (love's bowers)

Though such cunning them hath spread
None can part their white and red:
Love's golden arrows thence are shot,
Yet for them I love thee not.

I do not love thee for those soft,
Red coral lips I've kissed so oft;
Nor teeth of pearl, the double guard
To speech, whence music still is heard:
Though from those lips a kiss being taken,
Might tyrants melt and death awaken.

I do not love thee (O my fairest)
For that richest, for that rarest
Silver pillar which stands under
Thy round head, that globe of wonder;
Though that neck be whiter far,
Than towers of polished ivory are.

I do not love thee for those mountains
Hill'd with snow, whence milky fountains,
(Sugar'd sweet, as syrup't berries)
Must one day run through pipes of cherries;
O how much those breasts do move me,
Yet for them I do not love thee.

I do not love thee for that belly,
Sleek as satin, soft as jelly,
Though within that crystal round
Heaps of treasure might be found,
So rich that for the least of them,
A king might leave his diadem.

I do not love thee for those thighs
Whose alabaster rocks do rise
So high and even that they stand
Like sea-marks to some happy land.
Happy are those eyes have seen them,
More happy they that sail between them.

I love thee not for thy moist palm,
Though the dew thereof be balm:

Nor for thy pretty leg and foot,
Although it be the precious root,
On which this goodly cedar grows,
(Sweet) I love thee not for those.

Nor for thy wit though pure and quick,
Whose substance no arithmetic
Can number down: nor for those charms
Masked in thy embracing arms;
Though in them one night to lie,
Dearest I would gladly die.

I love not for those eyes, nor hair,
Nor cheeks, nor lips, nor teeth so rare;
Nor for thy speech, thy neck, nor breast,
Nor for thy belly, nor the rest:
Nor for thy hand, nor foot so small,
But wouldst thou know (dear sweet) for all.

A Rapture

I will enjoy thee now my Celia, come
    And fly with me to love's Elysium:
The giant, Honour, that keeps cowards out,
Is but a masquer, and the servile rout
Of baser subjects only, bend in vain
To the vast idol, whilst the nobler train
Of valiant lovers, daily sail between
The huge Colossus' legs, and pass unseen
Unto the blissful shore; be bold, and wise,
And we shall enter, the grim Swiss denies
Only tame fools a passage, that not know
He is but form, and only frights in show
The duller eyes that look from far; draw near,
And thou shalt scorn, what we were wont to fear.
We shall see how the stalking pageant goes
With borrowed legs, a heavy load to those
That made, and bear him; not as we once thought
The seeds of gods, but a weak model wrought

By greedy men, that seek to enclose the common,
And within private arms impale free woman.
    Come then, and mounted on the wings of love
We'll cut the flitting air, and soar above
The monster's head, and in the noblest seats
Of those blest shades, quench, and renew our heats.
There, shall the queen of love, and innocence,
Beauty and nature, banish all offence
From our close ivy twines, there I'll behold
Thy bared snow, and thy unbraided gold.
There, my enfranchised hand, on every side
Shall o'er thy naked polished ivory slide.
No curtain there, though of transparent lawn
Shall be before thy virgin-treasure drawn;
But the rich mine, to the enquiring eye
Exposed, shall ready still for mintage lie,
And we will coin young Cupids. There, a bed
Of roses, and fresh myrtles, shall be spread
Under the cooler shade of cypress groves:
Our pillows, of the down of Venus doves
Whereon our panting limbs we'll gently lay
In the faint respites of our active play;
That so our slumbers, may in dreams have leisure,
To tell the nimble fancy our past pleasure;
And so our souls that cannot be embraced,
Shall the embraces of our bodies taste.
Meanwhile the bubbling stream shall court the shore,
Th'enamoured chirping woodquire shall adore
In varied tunes the deity of love;
The gentle blasts of western winds shall move
The trembling leaves and through their close bows breath
Still music, whilst we rest ourselves beneath
Their dancing shade; till a soft murmur, sent
From souls entranced in amorous languishment
Rouse us, and shoot into our veins fresh fire,
Till we, in their sweet ecstasy expire.
    Then, as the empty bee, that lately bore,
Into the common treasure, all her store,

Flies 'bout the painted field with nimble wing,
Deflowering the fresh virgins of the Spring;
So will I rifle all the sweets, that dwell
In my delicious paradise, and swell
My bag with honey, drawn forth by the power
Of fervent kisses, from each spicy flower.
I'll seize the rosebuds in their perfumed bed,
The violet knots, like curious mazes spread
O'er all the garden, taste the ripened cherry,
The warm, firm apple, tipped with coral berry:
Then will I visit, with a wandering kiss,
The vale of lillies, and the bower of bliss:
And where the beauteous region doth divide
Into two milky ways, my lips shall slide
Down those smooth allies, wearing as I go
A tract for lovers on the printed snow;
Thence climbing o'er the swelling Appenine,
Retire into thy grove of eglantine;
Where I will all those ravished sweets distill
Through love's alembic, and with chemic skill
From the mixed mass, one sovereign balm derive,
Then bring that great elixir to thy hive.
    Now in more subtle wreaths I will entwine
My sinewy thighs, my legs and arms with thine;
Thou like a sea of milk shall lie displayed,
While I the smooth, calm ocean, invade
With such a tempest, as when Jove of old
Fell down on Danae in a storm of gold:
Yet my tall pine, shall in the Cyprian strait
Ride safe at anchor, and unload her freight:
My rudder, with thy bold hand, like a tried
And skilful pilot, thou shalt steer, and guide
My bark into love's channel, where it shall
Dance, as the bounding waves do rise or fall:
Then shall thy circling arms, embrace and clip
My willing body, and thy balmy lip
Bathe me in juice of kisses, whose perfume
Like a religious incense shall consume

And send up holy vapours, to those powers
That bless our loves, and crown our sportful hours,
That with such halcyon calmness, fix our souls
In steadfast peace, as no affright controls.
There, no rude sounds shake us with sudden starts,
No jealous ears, when we unrip our hearts
Suck our discourse in, no observing spies
This blush, that glance traduce; no envious eyes
Watch our close meetings, nor are we betrayed
To rivals, by the bribed chambermaid.
No wedlock bonds unwreath our twisted loves;
We seek no midnight arbor, no dark groves
To hide our kisses, there, the hated name
Of husband, wife, lust, modest, chaste, or shame,
Are vain and empty words, whose very sound
Was never heard in the Elysian ground.
All things are lawful there, that may delight
Nature, or unrestrained appetite;
Like, and enjoy, to will, and act, is one,
We only sin when love's rotes are not done.
    The Roman Lucrece there, reads the divine
Lectures of love's great master, Aretine,
And knows as well as Lais, how to move
Her pliant body in the act of love.
To quench the burning ravisher, she hurls
Her limbs into a thousand winding curls,
And studies artful postures, such as be
Carved on the bark of every neighbouring tree
By learned hands, that so adorned the rind
Of those fair plants, which as they lay entwined,
Have fanned their glowing fires. The Grecian dame,
That in her endless web, toiled for a name
As fruitless as her work, doth there display
Herself before the youth of Ithaca,
And th'amorous sport of gamesome nights prefer,
Before dull dreams of the lost traveller.
Daphne hath broke her bark, and that swift foot,
Which th'angry gods had fastened with a root

To the fixed earth, doth now unfettered run,
To meet th'embraces of the youthful sun:
She hangs upon him, like his Delphic lyre,
Her kisses blow the old, and breath new fire:
Full of her god, she sings inspired lays,
Sweet odes of love, such as deserve the bays,
Which she herself was. Next her, Laura lies
In Petrarch's learned arms, drying those eyes
That did in such sweet smooth-paced numbers flow,
As made the world enamoured of his woe.
These, and ten thousand beauties more, that died
Slave to the tyrant, now enlarged, deride
His cancelled laws, and for their time mispent,
Pay into love's exchequer double rent.
   Come then my Celia, we'll no more forbear
To taste our joys, struck with a panic fear,
But will depose from his imperious sway
This proud usurper and walk free, as they
With necks unyoked; nor is it just that he
Should fetter your soft sex with chastity,
Which nature made unapt for abstinence;
When yet this false imposter can dispense
With human justice, and with sacred right
And maugre both their laws command me fight
With rivals, or with emulous loves, that dare
Equal with thine, their mistress' eyes, or hair:
If thou complain of wrong, and call my sword
To carve out thy revenge, upon that word
He bids me fight and kill, or else he brands
With marks of infamy my coward hands,
And yet religion bids from bloodshed fly,
And damns me for that act. Then tell me why
This goblin Honour which the world adores,
Should make men atheists, and not women whores?

Edmund Waller
1606–87

On a Girdle

That which her slender waist confined,
Shall now my joyful temples bind;
No monarch but would give his crown
His arms might do what this has done.

It is my heaven's extremest sphere,
The pale which held the lovely dear,
My joy, my grief, my hope, my love,
Do all within this circle move.

A narrow compass, and yet there
Dwells all that's good, and all that's fair:
Give me but what this ribbon tied,
Take all the sun goes round beside.

John Milton
1608–74

from *L'Allegro*

There on beds of violets blue,
And fresh-blown roses washed in dew,
Filled her with thee a daughter fair,
So bucksome, blithe, and debonair.

from *Paradise Lost* (*Book IV*)

She as a veil down to the slender waist
Her unadorned golden tresses wore
Dishevelled, but in wanton ringlets waved
As the vine curls her tendrils, which implied
Subjection, but required with gentle sway,

And by her yielded, by him best received,
Yielded with coy submission, modest pride,
And sweet reluctant amorous delay.

from *Samson Agonistes*

Yet beauty, though injurious, hath strange power,
After offence returning, to regain
Love once possessed, nor can be easily
Repulsed without much inward passion felt
And secret sting of amorous remorse.

Sir John Suckling
1609–42

A Candle

There is a thing which in the light
Is seldom used, but in the night
It serves the maiden female crew,
The ladies, and the good-wives too:
They use to take it in their hand,
And then it will uprightly stand;
And to a hole they it apply,
Where by its good will it would die:
It spends, goes out, and still within
It leaves its moisture thick and thin.

The Deformed Mistress

I know there are some fools that care
Not for the body, so the face be fair:
Some others too that in a female creature
Respect not beauty, but a comely feature:
And others too, that for those parts in sight
Care not so much, so that the rest be right.

Each man his humour hath; and faith 'tis mine
To love that woman which I now define.
First I would have her wainscot face and hand
More wrinkled far than any plaited band,
That in those furrows, if I'd take the pains,
I might both sow and reap all sorts of grains:
Her nose I'd have a foot long, not above,
With pimples embroidered, for those I love;
And at the end a comely pearl of snot,
Considering whether it should fall or not:
Provided next that half her teeth be out,
I do not care much if her pretty snout
Meet with her furrowed chin, and both together
Hem in her lips, as dry as good white leather:
One wall-eye she shall have; for that's a sign
In other beasts the best, why not in mine?
Her neck I'll have to be pure jet at least,
With yellow spots enammelled; and her breast
Like a grasshopper's wing both thin and lean,
Not to be touched for dirt, unless swept clean:
As for her belly, 'tis no matter, so
There be a belly, and a cunt below;
Yet if you will, let it be something high,
And always let there be a timpanie.
But soft, where am I now! here I should stride,
Lest I fall in, the place must be so wide;
And pass unto her thighs, which shall be just
Like to an ant's that's scraping in the dust:
Into her legs I'd have love's issues fall,
And all her calf into a gouty small:
Her feet both thick, and eagle-like displayed,
The symptoms of a comely handsome maid.
As for her parts behind, I ask no more
If they but answer those that are before,
I have my utmost wish; and having so,
Judge whether I am happy, yea or no.

Alexander Brome

1620–66

To a Painted Lady

Leave these deluding tricks and shows,
    Be honest and downright:
What nature did to view expose,
    Don't you keep out of sight.
The novice youth may chance admire
    Your dressings, paints and spells:
But we that are expert desire
    Your sex for somewhat else.

In your adored face and hair,
    What virtue could you find,
If women were like angels fair,
    And every man were blind?
You need no pains or time to waste
    To set your beauties forth,
With oils, and paints and drugs, that cost
    More than the face is worth.

Nature herself, her own work does
    And hates all needless arts,
And all your artificial shows
    Disgrace your natural parts.
You're flesh and blood and so are we,
    Let flesh and blood alone,
To love all compounds hateful be,
    Give me the pure, or none.

Andrew Marvell
1621–78

To his Coy Mistress

Had we but world enough, and time,
This coyness lady were no crime.
We would sit down, and think which way
To walk, and pass our long love's day.
Thou by the Indian Ganges' side
Should'st rubies find: I by the tide
Of Humber would complain. I would
Love you ten years before the Flood:
And you should if you please refuse
Till the conversion of the Jews.
My vegetable love should grow
Vaster than empires, and more slow.
An hundred years should go to praise
Thine eyes, and on thy forehead gaze.
Two hundred to adore each breast:
But thirty thousand to the rest.
An age at least to every part,
And the last age should show your heart.
For lady you deserve this state;
Nor would I love at lower rate.
   But at my back I always hear
Time's winged chariot hurrying near:
And yonder all before us lie
Deserts of vast eternity.
Thy beauty shall no more be found;
Nor, in thy marble vault, shall sound
My echoing song: then worms shall try
That long preserved virginity:
And your quaint honour turn to dust;
And into ashes all my lust.
The grave's a fine and private place,
But none I think do there embrace.
   Now therefore, while the youthful hue
Sits on thy skin like morning dew,

And while thy willing soul transpires
At every pore with instant fires,
Now let us sport us while we may;
And now, like amorous birds of prey,
Rather at once our time devour,
Than languish in his slow-chapt power.
Let us roll all our strength, and all
Our sweetness, up into one ball:
And tear our pleasures with rough strife,
Through the iron gates of life.
Thus, though we cannot make our sun
Stand still, yet we will make him run.

Charles Cotton
1630–87

A Paraphrase

The beauty that must me delight,
Must have a skin and teeth snow white:
Black arched brows, black sprightly eyes,
And a black beauty 'twixt her thighs;
Soft blushing cheeks, a person tall,
Long hair, long hands, and fingers small;
Short teeth; and feet that little are,
Dilated brows, and haunches fair;
Fine silken hair, lips full and red,
Small nose, with little breast and head:
All these in one, and that one kind
Would make a mistress to my mind.

Forbidden Fruit

Pish! 'tis an idle fond excuse,
And love, enraged by this abuse,
Is deaf to any longer truce.

My zeal, to lust you still impute,
And when I justify my suit,
You tell me, '*Tis Forbidden Fruit*.

What though your face be apple-round,
And with a rosy colour crowned?
Yet, sweet, it is no apple found.

Nor have you aught resembling more
That fatal fruit the tree once bore,
But that indeed your heart's a core.

'Tis true, the bliss that I would taste,
Is something lower than the waist,
And in your garden's centre placed.

A tree of life too, I confess,
Though but arbuscular in dress,
Yet not forbidden ne'ertheless.

It is a tempting golden tree,
Which all men must desire that see,
Though it concerned eternity.

Then, since those blessings are thine own,
Not subject to contrition,
Then, fairest, sweetest, grant me one.

Thy dragon, wrapped in drowsiness,
Ne'er thinks whose bed thy beauties bless,
Nor dreams of his Hesperides.

John Dryden

1631–1700

'*Why should a foolish marriage vow*' (from *Marriage à la Mode*)

Why should a foolish marriage vow
   Which long ago was made,
Oblige us to each other now
   When passion is decayed?
We loved, and we loved, as long as we could,
   Till our love was loved out in us both:
But our marriage is dead, when the pleasure is fled:
   'Twas pleasure first made it an oath.

A New Song

Sylvia the fair, in the bloom of fifteen,
Felt an innocent warmth, as she lay on the green;
She had heard of a pleasure, and something she guessed
By the towzing and tumbling and touching her breast;
She saw the men eager, but was at a loss,
What they meant by their sighing, and kissing so close;
    By their praying and whining
    And clasping and twining,
    And panting and wishing,
    And sighing and kissing
    And sighing and kissing so close.

'Ah,' she cried, 'ah for a languishing maid
In a country of Christians to die without aid!
Not a Whig, or a Tory, or trimmer at least,
Or a Protestant parson, or Catholic priest,
To instruct a young virgin, that is at a loss
What they meant by their sighing, and kissing so close!'
    By their praying and whining
    And clasping and twining,
    And panting and wishing,
    And sighing and kissing
    And sighing and kissing so close.

Cupid in shape of a swain did appear,
He saw the sad wound, and in pity drew near,
Then showed her his arrow, and bid her not fear,
For the pain was no more than a maiden may bear;
When the balm was infused she was not at a loss,
What they meant by their sighing and kissing so close;
    By their praying and whining,
    And clasping and twining,
    And panting and wishing,
    And sighing and kissing
    And sighing and kissing so close.

Song for a Girl (from *Love Triumphant*)

Young I am, and yet unskilled
How to make a lover yield:
How to keep, or how to gain,
When to love; and when to feign:

Take me, take me, some of you,
While I yet am young and true;
E're I can my soul disguise;
Heave my breasts, and roll my eyes.

Stay not till I learn the way,
How to lie, and to betray;
He that has me first, is blest,
For I may deceive the rest.

Could I find a blooming youth;
Full of love, and full of truth,
Brisk, and of a jaunty mien,
I should long to be fifteen.

Sir Charles Sedley

1639–1701

On the Happy Corydon and Phyllis

Young Corydon and Phyllis
   Sat in a lovely grove,
Contriving crowns of lilies,
   Repeating toys of love,
And something else, but what I dare not name.

But as they were a-playing,
   She ogled so the swain;
It saved her plainly saying
   Let's kiss to ease our pain:
And something else, but what I dare not name.

A thousand times he kissed her,
   Laying her on the green;
But as he farther pressed her,
   A pretty leg was seen:
And something else, but what I dare not name.

So many beauties viewing,
   His ardour still increased;
And greater joys pursuing,
   He wandered o'er her breast:
And something else, but what I dare not name.

A last effort she trying,
   His passion to withstand;
Cried, but it was faintly crying,
   Pray take away your hand:
And something else, but what I dare not name.

Young Corydon grown bolder,
   The minutes would improve;
This is the time, he told her,
   To show you how I love;
And something else, but what I dare not name.

The nymph seemed almost dying,
    Dissolved in amorous heat;
She kissed and told him sighing,
    My dear your love is great:
And something else, but what I dare not name.

But Phyllis did recover
    Much sooner than the swain;
She blushing asked her lover,
    Shall we not kiss again:
And something else, but what I dare not name.

Thus Love his revels keeping,
    'Til Nature at a stand;
From talk they fell to sleeping,
    Holding each others hand;
And something else, but what I dare not name.

Aphra Behn
1640–89

'In a cottage'

In a cottage by the mountain
Lives a very pretty maid,
Who lay sleeping by a fountain
Underneath a myrtle shade;
Her petticoat of wanton sarcenet
The amorous wind about did move
And quite unveiled
And quite unveiled the throne of love
And quite unveiled the throne of love.

John Wilmot, Earl of Rochester

1647–80

The Imperfect Enjoyment

Naked she lay, clasped in my longing arms,
I filled with love, and she all over charms;
Both equally inspired with eager fire,
Melting through kindness, flaming in desire.
With arms, legs, lips close clinging to embrace,
She clips me to her breast, and sucks me to her face.
Her nimble tongue, Love's lesser lightning, played
Within my mouth, and to my thoughts conveyed
Swift orders that I should prepare to throw
The all-dissolving thunderbolt below.
My fluttering soul, sprung with the pointed kiss,
Hangs hovering o'er her balmy brinks of bliss.
But whilst her busy hand would guide that part
Which should convey my soul up to her heart,
In liquid raptures I dissolve all o'er,
Melt into sperm, and spend at every pore.
A touch from any part of her had done't:
Her hand, her foot, her very look's a cunt.
    Smiling, she chides in a kind murmuring noise,
And from her body wipes the clammy joys,
When with a thousand kisses wandering o'er
My panting bosom, 'Is there then no more?'
She cries. 'All this to love and rapture's due;
Must we not pay a debt to pleasure too?'
    But I, the most forlorn, lost man alive,
To show my wished obedience vainly strive:
I sigh, alas! and kiss, but cannot swive.
Eager desires confound my first intent,
Succeeding shame does more success prevent,
And rage at last confirms me impotent.
Ev'n her fair hand, which might bid heat return
To frozen age, and make cold hermits burn,
Applied to my dead cinder, warms no more
Than fire to ashes could past flames restore.

Trembling, confused, despairing, limber, dry,
A wishing, weak, unmoving lump I lie.
This dart of love, whose piercing point, oft tried,
With virgin blood ten thousand maids have dyed;
Which nature still directed with such art
That it through every cunt reached every heart –
Stiffly resolved, 'twould carelessly invade
Woman or man, nor ought its fury stayed:
Where'er it pierced, a cunt it found or made –
Now languid lies in this unhappy hour,
Shrunk up and sapless like a withered flower.

    Thou treacherous, base deserter of my flame,
False to my passion, fatal to my fame,
Through what mistaken magic dost thou prove
So true to lewdness, so untrue to love?
What oyster-cinder-beggar-common whore
Didst thou e'er fail in all thy life before?
When vice, disease, and scandal lead the way,
With what officious haste dost thou obey!
Like a rude, roaring hector in the streets
Who scuffles, cuffs, and justles all he meets,
But if his King or country claim his aid,
The rakehell villain shrinks and hides his head;
Ev'n so thy brutal valour is displayed,
Breaks every stew,[19] does each small whore invade,
But when great Love the onset does command,
Base recreant to thy prince, thou dar'st not stand.
Worse part of me, and henceforth hated most,
Through all the town a common fucking post,
On whom each whore relieves her tingling cunt
As hogs on gates do rub themselves and grunt,
Mayst thou to ravenous chancres be a prey,   *ulcers*
Or in consuming weepings[20] waste away;
May strangury and stone[21] thy days attend;
May'st thou ne'er piss, who didst refuse to spend
When all my joys did on false thee depend.

    And may ten thousand abler pricks agree
    To do the wronged Corinna right for thee.

Much wine had passed, with grave discourse
Of who fucks who, and who does worse
(Such as you usually do hear
From those that diet at the Bear[22]),
When I, who still take care to see
Drunkenness relieved by lechery,
Went out into St James's Park
To cool my head and fire my heart.
But though St James has th'honour on't,
'Tis consecrate to prick and cunt.
There, by a most incestuous birth,
Strange woods spring from the teeming earth;
For they relate how heretofore,
When ancient Pict began to whore,
Deluded of his assignation
(Jilting, it seems, was then in fashion),
Poor pensive lover, in this place
Would frig upon his mother's face;
Where rows of mandrakes tall did rise
Whose lewd tops fucked the very skies.
Each imitative branch does twine
In some loved fold of Aretine,[23]
And nightly now beneath their shade
Are buggeries, rapes, and incests made.
Unto this all-sin-sheltering grove
Whores of the bulk[24] and the alcove,
Great ladies, chambermaids, and drudges,
The ragpicker, and heiress trudges.
Carmen[25], divines, great lords, and tailors,
Prentices, poets, pimps, and jailers,
Footmen, fine fops do here arrive,
And here promiscuously they swive.

    Along these hallowed walks it was
That I beheld Corinna pass.
Whoever had been by to see
The proud disdain she cast on me

Through charming eyes, he would have swore
She dropped from heaven that very hour,
Forsaking the divine abode
In scorn of some despairing god.
But mark what creatures women are:
How infinitely vile, when fair!
    Three knights o'th'elbow and the slur[26]
With wriggling tails made up to her.
    The first was of your Whitehall blades,
Near kin t'th'Mother of the Maids[27];
Graced by whose favour he was able
To bring a friend t'th'Waiters' table,
Where he had heard Sir Edward Sutton[28]
Say how the King loved Banstead[29] mutton;
Since when he'd ne'er be brought to eat
By 's good will any other meat.
In this, as well as all the rest,
He ventures to do like the best,
But wanting common sense, th'ingredient
In choosing well not least expedient,
Converts abortive imitation
To universal affectation.
Thus he not only eats and talks
But feels and smells, sits down and walks,
Nay looks, and lives, and loves by rote,
In an old tawdry birthday coat.
    The second was a Grays Inn wit,
A great inhabiter of the pit,
Where critic-like he sits and squints,
Steals pocket handkerchiefs and hints,
From 's neighbour, and the comedy,
To court, and pay, his landlady.
    The third, a lady's eldest son
Within a few years of twenty-one,
Who hopes from his propitious fate,
Against he comes to his estate,
By these two worthies to be made
A most accomplished tearing blade.

One, in a strain 'twixt tune and nonsense,
Cries, 'Madam, I have loved you long since.
Permit me your fair hand to kiss;'
When at her mouth her cunt cries, 'Yes!'
In short, without much more ado,
Joyful and pleased, away she flew,
And with these three confounded asses
From park to hackney coach she passes.
    So a proud bitch does lead about
Of humble curs the amorous rout,
Who most obsequiously do hunt
The savoury scent of salt-swoln cunt.
Some power more patient now relate
The sense of this surprising fate.
Gods! that a thing admired by me
Should fall to so much infamy.
Had she picked out, to rub her arse on,
Some stiff-pricked clown or well-hung parson,
Each job[30] of whose spermatic sluice
Had filled her cunt with wholesome juice,
I the proceeding should have praised
In hope sh'had quenched a fire I raised.
Such natural freedoms are but just:
There's something generous in mere lust.
But to turn damned abandoned jade
When neither head nor tail persuade;
To be a whore in understanding,
A passive pot for fools to spend in!
The devil played booty,[31] sure, with thee
To bring a blot on infamy.
    But why am I, of all mankind,
To so severe a fate designed?
Ungrateful! Why this treachery
To humble, fond, believing me,
Who gave you privilege above
The nice allowances of love?
Did ever I refuse to bear
The meanest part your lust could spare?

When your lewd cunt came spewing home
Drenched with the seed of half the town,
My dram of sperm was supped up after
For the digestive surfeit water.[32]
Full gorgèd at another time
With a vast meal of nasty slime
Which your devouring cunt had drawn
From porters' backs and footmen's brawn,
I was content to serve you up
My ballock-full for your grace cup,
Nor ever thought it an abuse
While you had pleasure for excuse –
You that could make my heart away
For noise and colour, and betray
The secrets of my tender hours
To such knight-errant paramours,
When, leaning on your faithless breast,
Wrapped in security and rest,
Soft kindness all my powers did move,
And reason lay dissolved in love!

   May stinking vapours choke your womb
Such as the men you dote upon!
May your depraved appetite,
That could in whiffling fools delight,
Beget such frenzies in your mind
You may go mad for the north wind,
And fixing all your hopes upon't
To have him bluster in your cunt,
Turn up your longing arse t'th'air
And perish in a wild despair!
But cowards shall forget to rant,
Schoolboys to frig, old whores to paint;
The Jesuits' fraternity
Shall leave the use of buggery;
Crab-louse, inspired with grace divine,
From earthly cod to heaven shall climb;
Physicians shall believe in Jesus,
And disobedience cease to please us,

Ere I desist with all my power
To plague this woman and undo her.
But my revenge will best be timed
When she is married that is limed.
In that most lamentable state
I'll make her feel my scorn and hate:
Pelt her with scandals, truth or lies,
And her poor cur with jealousies,
Till I have torn him from her breech,
While she whines like a dog-drawn bitch;
Loathed and despised, kicked out o'th'Town
Into some dirty hole alone,
To chew the cud of misery
And know she owes it all to me.
    And may no woman better thrive
    That dares profane the cunt I swive!

Signior Dildo[33]

You ladies all of merry England
Who have been to kiss the Duchess's hand,
Pray, did you lately observe in the show
A noble Italian called Signior Dildo?

This signior was one of Her Highness's train,
And helped to conduct her over the main;
But now she cries out, 'To the Duke I will go!
I have no more need for Signior Dildo.'

At the Sign of the Cross in St James's Street,
When next you go hither to make yourselves sweet
By buying of powder, gloves, essence, or so,
You may chance t'get a sight of Signior Dildo.

You'll take him at first for no person of note
Because he appears in a plain leather coat,
But when you his virtuous abilities know,
You'll fall down and worship Signior Dildo.

My Lady Southesk, heavens prosper her for't!
First clothed him in satin, then brought him to Court;
But his head in the circle he scarcely durst show,
So modest a youth was Signior Dildo.

The good Lady Suffolk, thinking no harm,
Had got this poor stranger hid under her arm.
Lady Betty by chance came the secret to know,
And from her own mother stole Signior Dildo.

The Countess of Falmouth, of whom people tell
Her footmen wear shirts of a guinea an ell,
Might save the expense if she did but know
How lusty a swinger is Signior Dildo.

By the help of this gallant the countess of Ralph
Against the fierce Harrys preserved herself safe.
She stifled him almost beneath her pillow,
So closely sh'embraced Signior Dildo.

Our dainty fine duchesses have got a trick
To dote on a fool for the sake of his prick:
The fops were undone, did Their Graces but know
The discretion and vigour of Signior Dildo.

That pattern of virtue, Her Grace of Cleveland,
Has swallowed more pricks than the ocean has sand;
But by rubbing and scrubbing so large it does grow,
It is fit for just nothing but Signior Dildo.

The Duchess of Modena, though she looks high,
With such a gallant is contented to lie,
And for fear the English her secrets should know,
For a Gentleman Usher took Signior Dildo.

The countess o'th'Cockpit (Who knows not her name?
She's famous in story for a killing dame),
When all her old lovers forsake her, I trow
She'll then be contented with Signior Dildo.

Red Howard, red Sheldon, and Temple so tall
Complain of his absence so long from Whitehall;
Signior Bernard has promised a journey to go
And bring back his countryman Signior Dildo.

Doll Howard no longer with 's Highness must range,
And therefore is proffered this civil exchange:
Her teeth being rotten, she smells best below,
And needs must be fitted for Signior Dildo.

St Albans, with wrinkles and smiles in his face,
Whose kindness to strangers becomes his high place,
In his coach and six horses is gone to Borgo
To take the fresh air with Signior Dildo.

Were this signior but known to the citizen fops,
He'd keep their fine wives from the foremen of shops;
But the rascals deserve their horns and should still grow
For burning the Pope and his nephew Dildo.

Tom Killigrew's wife, north Holland's fine flower,
At the sight of this signior did fart and belch sour,
And her Dutch breeding farther to show,
Says, 'Welcome to England, Mynheer van Dildo!'

He civilly came to the Cockpit one night,
And proffered his service to fair Madam Knight.
Quoth she, 'I intrigue with Captain Cazzo;
Your nose in mine arse, good Signior Dildo!'

This signior is sound, safe, ready, and dumb
As ever was candle, carrot, or thumb;
Then away with these nasty devices, and show
How you rate the just merits of Signior Dildo.

Count Cazzo, who carries his nose very high,
In passion he swore his rival should die;
Then shut up himself to let the world know
Flesh and blood could not bear it from Signior Dildo.

A rabble of pricks who were welcome before,
Now finding the Porter denied 'em the door,
Maliciously waited his coming below
And inhumanly fell on Signior Dildo.

Nigh wearied out, the poor stranger did fly,
And along the Pall Mall they followed full cry;
The women, concerned, from every window
Cried, 'Oh! for heaven's sake, save Signior Dildo!'

The good Lady Sandys burst into a laughter
To see how the ballocks came wobbling after,
And had not their weight retarded the foe,
Indeed't had gone hard with Signior Dildo.

To a Lady in a Letter

Such perfect bliss, fair Chloris, we
 In our enjoyments prove,
'Tis pity restless jealousy
 Should mingle with our love.

Let us, since wit has taught us how,
 Raise pleasure to the top:
You rival bottle must allow,
 I'll suffer rival fop.

Think not in this that I design
 A treason 'gainst love's charms,
When, following the god of wine,
 I leave my Chloris' arms,

Since you have that, for all your haste
 (At which I'll ne'er repine),
Will take its liquor off as fast
 As I can take off mine.

There's not a brisk, insipid spark
 That flutters in the town,
But with your wanton eyes you mark
 Him out to be your own;

Nor do you think it worth your care
 How empty and how dull
The heads of your admirers are,
 So that their cods be full.

All this you freely may confess,
 Yet we ne'er disagree,
For did you love your pleasure less,
 You were no match for me.

Whilst I, my pleasure to pursue,
   Whole nights am taking in
The lusty juice of grapes, take you
   The juice of lusty men.

On Cary Frazier[34]

Her father gave her dildoes six;
   Her mother made 'em up a score;
But she loves nought but living pricks,
   And swears by God she'll frig no more.

Anonymous
17th century

Love's Courtship

Hark my Flora, Love doth call us
To the strife that must befall us:
He hath robbed his mother's myrtles,
And hath pulled her downy turtles.
   See our genial posts are crowned,
And our beds like billows rise:
   Softer lists are nowhere found,
And the strife itself's the prize.

Let not shades and dark affright thee,
Thy eyes have lustre that will light thee:
Think not any can surprise us,
Love himself doth now disguise us:
   From thy waist that girdle throw
Night and silence both wait here,
   Words or actions who can know
Where there's neither eye nor ear.

Show thy bosom and then hide it,
License touching and then chide it;
Proffer something and forbear it,
Give a grant and then forswear it:

Ask where all my shame is gone,
Call us wanton wicked men;
    Do as turtles kiss and groan,
Say thou nere shalt joy again.

I can hear thee curse, yet chase thee;
Drink thy tears and still embrace thee:
Easy riches are no treasure,
She that's willing spoils the pleasure:
    Love bids learn the wrestler's sleight,
Pull and struggle when we twine;
    Let me use my force tonight,
The next conquest shall be thine.

On Love

    When I do love I would not wish to speed,
To plead fruition rather than desire,
    But on sweet lingering expectation feed,
And gently would protract not feed my fire.
    What though my love a martyrdom you name,
    No salamander ever feels the flame.

    That which is obvious I as much esteem
As courtiers do old clothes: for novelty
    Doth relish pleasures, and in them we deem
The hope is sweeter than the memory.
    Enjoying breeds a glut, men better taste
    Comforts to come, than pleasures that are past.

The Loose Wooer

Thou dost deny me 'cause thou art a wife.
Know, she that's married lives a single life
That loves but one. Abhor the nuptial curse,
Tied thee to him, for better and for worse.
Variety delights the active blood,
And women the more common, the more good,
As all goods are. There's no adultery,
And marriage is the worst monopoly.

The learned Roman clergy admits none
Of theirs to marry; they love all, not one.
And every nun can teach you, 'tis as meet
To change your bedfellows, as smock or sheet.
Say, would you be content only to eat
Mutton or beef, and taste no other meat?
   It would grow loathsome to you, and I know
   You have two palates, and the best below.

'Within this coffin'

Within this coffin, sinew-shrunk and dead,
Lies Doll's delight, and she no tear hath shed.
Not that she wants affection to lament
Th' entombing of so sweet an instrument
Of her content, but that her power is such
That she can raise it up, and with her touch
Make it so speak that he which understands
The language must confess her active hands
Have strength, though not the chain of fate to break,
Yet sure to raise the dead and make it speak.
And if you be impatient of delay
To know the mystery, then bid her play.

'Here six foot deep'

   Here six foot deep
   In his last sleep
The Lord of Lampas lies,
   Who his end made
   With his own blade
Between his mistress' thighs.

   If through that hole
   To heaven he stole,
I dare be bold to say
   He was the last
   Who that way passed
And first that found the way.

The Old Woman

Why should men that women know
Honour, love, respect them so,
If they knew their age or youth,
Which never knew nor good nor truth?

And what their youth did them allow,
In age they would, if they knew how.
In youth inconstant, so they'll end
In age the same: pray God they'll mend.

But they would mend if death would stay
And live they would till the last day,
And end their time in wanton sport,
And dying cry, 'Too short, too short!'

'Underneath this stone'

Underneath this stone and brick
Lies one that once loved well a prick.
All you that pass by, do her this honour:
Pull out your pintles and piss upon her.

Upon a Courtesan's Lute

Pretty lute, when I am gone
Tell thy mistress here was one
That hither came with full intent
To play upon her instrument.

Of a Forsworn Maid

Rosa being false and perjured, once a friend
Bid me contented be and mark her end.
But yet I care not. Let my friend go fiddle,
And let him mark her end: I'll mark her middle.

'My mistress is in music'

My mistress is in music passing skilful
And plays and sings her part at the first sight,
But in her play she is exceeding wilful
And will not play but for her own delight,
Nor touch one string nor play one pleasing strain
Unless you catch her in a merry vein.

Also she hath a sweet delicious touch
Upon the instrument whereon she plays,
And thinks that she doth never do too much,
Her pleasure is dispersed so many ways.
She hath such judgement both in time and mood
That for to play with her, 'twill do you good.

And then you win her heart. But here's the spite:
You cannot get her for to play alone.
But play you with her, and she plays all night,
And next day too, or else 'tis ten to one;
And runs division with you in such sort,
Run ne'er so swift, she'll make you come too short.

One day she called me for to come and play
And I did hold it an exceeding grace;
But she so tired me ere I went away
I wished I had been in another place.
She knew the place where prick and rest both stood
Yet would she keep no time for life nor blood.

I love my mistress, and I love to play,
So she will let me play with intermission.
But when she ties me to it all the day
I hate and loathe her greedy disposition.
Let her keep time, as nature doth require,
And I will play as long as she desire.

'Walking in a meadow'

Walking in a meadow green,
    Fair flowers for to gather,
Where primrose ranks did stand on banks
    To welcome comers thither,
I heard a voice that made a noise,
    Which caused me to attend it.
I heard a lass say to a lad,
    'Once more, and none can mend it.'

They two did lie so close together
    They made me much to wonder.
I thought he would this nymph quite smother
    Whenas I saw her under.
Then off he came and blushed for shame,
    That he so soon had ended.
Yet still she lies and to him cries,
    'Once more, and none can mend it.'

His looks were dull and very sad;
    His courage she had tamèd.
She bade him play the lusty lad
    Or else he quite was shamèd.
'Then stiffly thrust and hit me just.
    Fear not, but freely spend it
And play a bout at in and out
    Once more, and none can mend it.'

Then in her arms she did him fold
    And oftentimes she kissed him,
Yet still his courage was but cold
    For all the good she wished him.
Then with her hand she made it stand
    So stiff she could not bend it,
And then anon she cries, 'Come on!
    Once more, and none can mend it.'

And then he thought to venture her,
    Thinking the fit was on him,
But when he came to enter her
    The point turned back upon him.

Yet she said, 'Stay! Go not away
    Although the point be bended!
But to't again, and hit the vein!
    Once more, and none can mend it.'

'Adieu, adieu, sweetheart,' quoth he,
    'For in faith I must be gone.'
'Nay then, you do me wrong,' quoth she,
    'To leave me thus alone.'
Away he went when all was spent,
    Whereat she was offended.
Like a Trojan true she made a vow
    She would have one should mend it.

'*I dreamed my love*'

I dreamed my love lay in her bed
    And 'twas my chance to take her.
Her arms and legs abroad were spread.
    She slept, I durst not wake her.

O pity it were that one so fair
    Should crown her head with willow.
The tresses of her golden hair
    Did kiss her lovely pillow.

Me thought her belly was a hill
    Much like a mount of pleasure,
At foot whereof there springs a well,
    The depth no man can measure.

About the pleasant mountain head
    There grew a lovely thicket,
Whither two beagles travellèd
    And raised a lively pricket.

They hunted him with cheerful cry
    About this pleasant mountain,
That he with heat was forced to fly
    And slip into the fountain.

Those beagles followed to the brink
   And there at him they baited.
He plunged about but would not shrink.
   His coming-forth they waited.

Then forth he came as one half lame,
   Full weary, faint and tired,
And laid him down between her legs
   As help he had required.

Those beagles being refreshed again,
   My love from sleep bereaved.
She dreamed she had me in her arms
   And she was not deceived.

A Riddle

Come, pretty nymph, fain would I know
What thing it is that breeds delight,
That strives to stand, and cannot go,
And feeds the mouth that cannot bite.

It is a kind of pleasing thing,
A pricking and a piercing sting.
It is Venus' wanton wand.
It hath no legs and yet can stand.
A bachelor's button thoroughly ripe,
The kindest new tobacco pipe.
It is the pen that Helen took
To write in her two-leavèd book.
It's a prick-shaft of Cupid's cut,
Yet some do shoot it at a butt.
And every wench by her good will
Would keep it in her quiver still.
The fairest yet that e'er had life
For love of this became a wife.

A Riddle of a Gooseberry

There is a bush fit for the nonce
That beareth pricks and pretty stones.
The fruit in fear some ladies pull,
'Tis smooth and round and plump and full.
It yields dear moisture, pure and thick.
It seldom makes a lady sick.

They put it in, and then they move it,
Which makes it melt, and then they love it.
So what was round, plump, full and hard
Grows lank and thin and dull and marred.
The sweetness sucked, they wipe and stay,
And throw the empty skin away.

A Mistress

Her for a mistress would I fain enjoy
That hangs the lip and pouts at every toy;
Speaks like a wag; is fair; dare boldly stand
And rear love's standard with a wanton hand;
That in love's fight for one blow gives me three,
And being stabbed, falls straight a-kissing me;
For if she want those tricks of venery
Were't Venus' self, I could not love her, I.
    If she be modest, wise and chaste of life,
    Hang her! she's fit for nothing but a wife.

'She lay all naked'

She lay all naked on her bed
    And I myself lay by;
No veil but curtains round her spread,
    No covering but I.

Her head upon one shoulder seeks
    To lean in careless wise.
All full of blushes were her cheeks,
    Of wishes were her eyes.

The blood still flushing in her face
　　As on a message came
To show that in another place
　　It meant another game.

Her cherry lips, soft, sweet and fair
　　Millions of kisses crown,
Which ripe and uncropped dangle there
　　And weigh the branches down.

Her breast that swelled so plump and high
　　Bred pleasant pain in me,
That all the world I would defy
　　For that felicity.

Her thighs and belly soft and neat
　　To me were only shown.
To have seen such meat and not have eat
　　Would have angered any stone.

Her knees lay up and gently bent
　　And all was hollow under,
As if on easy terms they meant
　　To fall unforced asunder.

Just so the Cyprian dame[35] did lie
　　Expecting in her bower
When too long sport had kept the boy
　　Beyond his promised hour.

'Dull clown,' said she, 'that dost delay
　　This proffered bliss to take!
Canst thou not find a sweeter way
　　Similitudes to make?'

Mad with delight I thundered in
　　And threw my arms about her.
But pox upon't! I waked agin
　　And there I lay without her.

'Johnny took Joan'

Johnny took Joan by the arm
And led her unto the haycock;
And yet he did her no harm,
Although he felt under her smock.
  Although he did touse her,
  Although he did rouse her
Until she backwards did fall,
  She did not complain
  Nor his kindness refrain,
But prayed him to put it in all.

'*Last night I dreamed*'

Last night I dreamed of my love
When sleep did overtake her.
It was a pretty, drowsy rogue;
She slept; I durst not wake her.

Her lips were like to coral red;
A thousand times I kissed 'um,
And a thousand times more I might have stol'n,
For she had ne'er missed 'um.

Her crisped locks, like threads of gold,
Hung dangling o'er the pillow;
Great pity 'twas that one so fair
Should wear the rainbow-willow.

I folded down the holland sheet
A little below her belly,
But what I did you ne'er shall know,
Nor is it meet to tell ye.

Her belly's like to yonder hill –
Some call it Mount of Pleasure –
And underneath there springs a well
Which no man's depth can measure.

Thomas D'Urfey

1653–1723

A Song

The night her blackest sables wore,
   And gloomy were the skies;
And glittering stars there were no more,
   Than those in Stella's eyes:
When at her father's gate I knocked,
   Where I had often been,
And shrouded only with her smock,
   The fair one let me in.

Fast locked within my close embrace,
   She trembling lay ashamed;
Her swelling breast, and glowing face,
   And every touch inflamed:
My eager passion I obeyed,
   Resolved the fort to win;
And her fond heart was soon betrayed,
   To yield and let me in.

Then! then! beyond expressing,
   Immortal was the joy;
I knew no greater blessing,
   So great a god was I:
And she transported with delight,
   Oft prayed me come again;
And kindly vowed that every night,
   She'd rise and let me in.

But, oh! at last she proved with bairn,
   And sighing sat and dull;
And I that was a much concerned,
   Looked then just like a fool:
Her lovely eyes with tears run o'er,
   Repenting her rash sin;
She sighed and cursed the fatal hour,
   That e'er she let me in.

But who could cruelly deceive,
    Or from such beauty part;
I loved her so, I could not leave
    The charmer of my heart:
But wedded and concealed the crime,
    Thus all was well again;
And now she thanks the blessed time,
    That e'er she let me in.

Matthew Prior
1664–1721

A Lover's Anger

As Cloe came into the room t'other day,
I peevish began; 'Where so long could you stay?
In your lifetime you never regarded your hour:
You promised at two; and (pray look child) 'tis four.
A lady's watch needs neither figures nor wheels:
'Tis enough, that 'tis loaded with baubles and seals.
A temper so heedless no mortal can bear—'
Thus far I went on with a resolute air.
'Lord bless me!' said she; 'let a body but speak:
Here's an ugly hard rosebud fallen into my neck:
It has hurt me, and vexed me to such a degree –
See here; for you never believe me; pray see,
On the left side my breast what a mark it has made.'
So saying, her bosom she careless displayed.
That seat of delight I with wonder surveyed;
And forgot every word I designed to have said.

A True Maid

'No, no; for my virginity,
    When I lose that,' says Rose, 'I'll die;'
'Behind the elms, last night,' cried Dick,
    'Rose, were you not extremely sick?'

'Nanny blushes'

Nanny blushes, when I woo her,
   And with kindly chiding eyes,
Faintly says, I shall undo her,
   Faintly, O forbear, she cries.

But her breasts while I am pressing,
   While to her's my lips I join;
Warmed she seems to taste the blessing,
   And her kisses answer mine.

Undebauched by rules of honour,
   Innocence, with nature, charms;
One bids, gently push me from her,
   T'other take me in her arms.

Jonathan Swift
1667–1745

from *Cadenus and Vanessa*

That modern love is no such thing
As what those ancient poets sing;
A fire celestial, chaste, refined,
Conceived and kindled in the mind,
Which having found an equal flame,
Unites, and both become the same,
In different breasts together burn,
Together both to ashes turn.
But women now feel no such fire,
And only know the gross desire;
Their passions move in lower spheres,
Where-e'er caprice or folly steers.
A dog, a parrot, or an ape,
Or some worse brute in human shape,
Engross the fancies of the fair,
The few soft moments they can spare,

149

From visits to receive and pay,
From scandal, politics, and play,
From fans, and flounces, and brocades,
From equipage and park-parades,
From all the thousand female toys,
From every trifle that employs
The out or inside of their heads
Between their toilets and their beds.

Ambrose Philips
1675–1749

from *Ode to the Hon Miss Carteret*

Then the taper-moulded waist
With a span of riband braced,
And the swell of either breast,
And the wide high-vaulted chest,
And the neck so white and round,
Little neck with brilliants bound,
And the store of charms which shine
Above in lineaments divine,
Crowded in a narrow space
To complete the desperate face;
These alluring powers and more
Shall enamoured youths adore;
These and more in courtly lays
Many an aching heart shall praise.
    Happy thrice, and thrice again,
Happiest he of happy men
Who in courtship greatly sped
Wins the damsel to his bed,
Bears the virgin prize away
Counting life one nuptial day!

Elijah Fenton
1683–1730

Olivia

Olivia's lewd, but looks devout,
And scripture-proofs she throws about,
   When first you try to win her:
But pull your fob of guineas out;
Fee Jenny first, and never doubt
   To find the saint a sinner.

Baxter[36] by day is her delight:
No chocolate must come in sight
   Before two morning chapters:
But, lest the spleen should spoil her quite,
She takes a civil friend at night
   To raise her holy raptures.

Thus oft we see a glow-worm gay
At large her fiery tail display,
   Encouraged by the dark;
And yet the sullen thing all day
Snug in some lonely thicket lay,
   And hid the native spark.

Alexander Pope
1688–1744

from *Of The Characters of Women* (*Moral Essays:* Epistle 2)

Yet mark the fate of a whole sex of queens!
Power all their end, but beauty all the means:
In youth they conquer, with so wild a rage,
As leaves them scarce a subject in their age:
For foreign glory, foreign joy, they roam;
No thought of peace or happiness at home.

But wisdom's triumph is well-timed retreat,
As hard a science to the fair as great!
Beauties, like tyrants, old and friendless grown,
Yet hate repose, and dread to be alone,
Worn out in public, weary every eye,
Nor leave one sigh behind them when they die.

 Pleasure the sex, as children birds, pursue,
Still out of reach, yet never out of view;
Sure, if they catch, to spoil the toy at most,
To covet flying, and regret when lost:
At last, to follies youth could scarce defend,
It grows their age's prudence to pretend;
Ashamed to own they gave delight before,
Reduced to feign it, when they give no more:
As hags hold Sabbaths, less for joy than spite,
So these their merry, miserable night;
Still round and round the ghosts of beauty glide,
And haunt the places where their honour died.

Sauda
18th century

'He fixes his lady's bodice'

He fixes his lady's bodice with a stare,
'Tell me,' he asks, 'what have you got in there?
Are they two loaves? Or two delicious cheeses?'
Or, if his hand should stray into her breeches,
'What's this I feel,' he cries, 'So soft and warm?
Newly-baked bread? If so 'twould do no harm
To let me eat it. Why do you hide it from me?'

Edward Moore

1712–57

from *Fable*

Why, Celia, is your spreading waist
So loose, so negligently laced?
Why must the wrapping bedgown hide
Your snowy bosom's swelling pride?
How ill that dress adorns your head,
Distained and rumpled from the bed!
Those clouds that shade your blooming face
A little water might displace,
As nature every morn bestows
The crystal dew to cleanse the rose:
Those tresses, as the raven black,
That waved in ringlets down your back,
Uncombed and injured by neglect,
Destroy the face which once they decked.
     Whence this forgetfulness of dress?
Pray, madam, are you married? Yes.
Nay, then, indeed the wonder ceases;
No matter how loose your dress is;
The end is won, your fortune's made;
Your sister now may take the trade.

Anonymous

18th century

Have-at a Venture

The powers of love so powerful are,
 What mortal can withstand,
Or, who can say oppose they dare
 Where Cupid *bears command*
This damsel quickly she did yield
 The youngster's skill to try,
The twinkling Archer won the Field,
 And then she down did lie.

A country lad and bonny lass
   they did together meet
And as they did together pass
   thus he began to greet!
What I do say I may mind well,
   and thus I do begin:
If you would have your belly swell
   Hold up, and I'll put in.

Oh! Sir, (quoth she) I love the sport,
   Yet am afraid to try,
And for your love, I thank you for't,
   find but conveniency:
My mind I'll tell you by and by,
   your love my heart doth win,
And presently I down will lie,
   Oh! then Boy push it in.

He clasped this damsel round the waist
   and softly laid her down,
Yea wantonly he her embraced
   and her delights did crown:
Thrust home (quoth she) my brisk young lad,
   'Tis but a venial sin,
For I should soon have run quite mad
   had you not put it in.

The sport he did so close pursue
   that he was quickly tired;
But when he did her beauty view
   his heart again was fired:
He came on with such fresh supplies,
   he did her favour win,
And finding babies in her eyes,
   he bravely thrust it in.

What pleasure is there like to this,
   this damsel then did cry,
I've heard them talk of lovers' bliss,
   Oh! what a fool was I

So long to live a maid, ere I
   did this same sport begin;
This death I now could freely die:
   I prithee thrust it in.

She held this youngster to his task
   till he began to blow;
Then at the last he leave did ask
   and so she let him go:
Then down he panting lay awhile,
   and rousing up again
She charmed him with a lovely smile
   again to put it in.

To work he went most earnestly,
   her fancy to fulfill;
Till at the last she loud did cry,
   I do't with such good will,
I pleasure feel in every vein;
   my joys do now begin,
Oh dearest quickly to't again
   and stoutly thrust it in.

She seemed at last to be content,
   and glad at heart was he,
His youthful strength was almost spent,
   so brisk a lass was she:
He vowed he never was so matched,
   nor ne'er shall be again:
And for that time they both dispatched,
   though he had put it in.

But when she from him parted was
   Thus she began to cry,
Was ever any wanton lass
   in such a case as I:
He that hath got my maidenhead
   I ne'er shall see again,
And now my heart is almost dead,
   to think he put it in.

But yet it had the sweetest taste
    that ever mortal knew,
Our time we did not vainly waste,
    believe me this is true:
Should I e'er see my bonny lad,
    I'd venture once again,
And let the world account me mad,
    again I'll put it in.

The Wanton Trick

If anyone long for a musical song,
    Although that his hearing be thick,
The sound that it bears will ravish his ears,
    Whoop, 'tis but a wanton trick.

A pleasant young maid on an instrument played,
    That knew neither note, nor prick;
She had a good will to live by her skill,
    Whoop, 'tis but a wanton trick.

A youth in that art well seen in his part,
    They called him Derbyshire Dick,
Came to her a suitor, and would be her tutor,
    Whoop, 'tis but a wanton trick.

To run with his bow he was not slow,
    His fingers were nimble and quick,
When he played on his bass, he ravished the lass,
    Whoop, 'tis but a wanton trick.

He woo'd her and taught her, until he had brought her
    To hold out a crotchet and prick,
And by his direction, she came to perfection,
    Whoop, 'tis but a wanton trick.

With playing and wooing he still would be doing,
    And called her his pretty sweet chick:
His reasonable motion brought her to devotion,
    Whoop, 'tis but a wanton trick.

He pleased her so well, that backwards she fell,
　　And swooned, as though she were sick;
So sweet was his note, that up went her coat,
　　Whoop, 'tis but a wanton trick.

The string of his viol she put to the trial,
　　Till she had the full length of the stick;
Her white-bellied lute she set to his flute,
　　Whoop, 'tis but a wanton trick.

Thus she with her lute, and he with his flute,
　　Held every crotchet and prick;
She learned at leisure, yet paid for the pleasure,
　　Whoop, 'tis but a wanton trick.

His viol-string burst, her tutor she cursed,
　　However she played with the stick,
From October to June she was quite out of tune,
　　Whoop, 'tis but a wanton trick.

With shaming her hand to make the pin stand,
　　The music within her grew thick,
Of his viol and lute appeared some fruit,
　　Whoop, 'tis but a wanton trick.

And then she repented that e'er she consented,
　　To have either note or prick;
For learning so well made her belly to swell,
　　Whoop, 'tis but a wanton trick.

All maids that make trial of a lute or a viol,
　　Take heed how you handle the stick:
If you like not this order, come try my recorder,
　　Whoop, 'tis but a wanton trick.

And if this ditty forsooth doth not fit ye,
　　I know not what music to prick,
There's never a strain but in time will be twain,
　　Whoop, 'tis but a wanton trick.

The Maid's Conjuring Book

A young man lately in our town,
  He went to bed one night;
He had no sooner laid him down,
  But was troubled with a Sprite:
So vigorously the Spirit stood,
  Let him do what he can,
Sure then he said it must be laid,
  By woman not by man.

A handsome maid did undertake,
  And into bed she leapt;
And to allay the Spirit's power,
  Full close to him she crept:
She having such a guardian care,
  Her office to discharge;
She opened wide her conjuring book,
  And laid the leaves at large.

Her office she did well perform,
  Within a little space;
Then up she rose, and down he lay,
  And durst not show his face;
She took her leave, and away she went,
  When she had done the deed;
Saying, 'If't chance to come again,
  Then send for me with speed.'

The Mower

It was one summer's morning on the fourteenth day of May,
I met a fair maid, she asked my trade, I made her this reply,
For by my occupation I ramble up and down,
With my taring scythe in order to mow the meadows down.

She said, my handsome young man, if a mower that you be,
I'll find you some new employment if you will go with me,
For I have a little meadow long kept for you in store,
It was on the dew, I tell you true, it ne'er was cut before.

He said, my pretty fair maid, if it is as you say,
I'll do my best endeavours in cutting of your hay,
For in your lovely countenance I never saw a frown,
So my lovely lass, I'll cut your grass, that's ne'er been trampled
    down.

With courage bold undaunted she took him to the ground,
With his taring scythe in hand to mow the meadow down;
He mowed from nine till breakfast time, so far beyond his skill,
He was forced to yield and quit the field, for the grass was growing
    still.

She says, my handsome young man, you did promise me and say
You'd do your best endeavours in cutting of the hay,
For in my little meadow, you'll ne'er find hills nor rocks,
So I pray young man don't leave me, till you see my hay in cocks.

He said, my pretty fair maid, I can no longer stay,
But I'll go to Newry, in cutting of the hay,
But if I find the grass is cut in the country where I go,
It's then perhaps I may return, your meadow for to mow.

Now her hay being in order, and harvest being all o'er,
This young man's gone and left her sad case for to deplore,
But where he's gone I do not know, so far beyond my skill,
I was forced to yield and quit the field, for grass is growing still.

Richard Brinsley Sheridan
1751–1816

The Geranium

In the close covert of a grove,
By nature formed for scenes of love,
Said Susan in a lucky hour,
Observe yon sweet geranium flower;
How straight upon its stalk it stands,
And tempts our violating hands:

Whilst the soft bud as yet unspread,
Hangs down its pale declining head:
Yet, soon as it is ripe to blow,
The stems shall rise, the head shall glow.
Nature, said I, my lovely Sue,
To all her followers lends a clue;
Her simple laws themselves explain,
As links of one continued chain;
For her the mysteries of creation,
Are but the works of generation:
Yon blushing, strong triumphant flower,
Is in the crisis of its power:
But short, alas! its vigorous reign,
He sheds his seed, and drops again;
The bud that hangs in pale decay,
Feels, not, as yet, the plastic ray;
Tomorrow's sun shall bid him rise,
Then, too, he sheds his seed and dies:
But words, my love, are vain and weak,
For proof, let bright example speak;
Then straight before the wondering maid,
The tree of life I gently laid;
Observe, sweet Sue, his drooping head,
How pale, how languid, and how dead;
Yet, let the sun of thy bright eyes,
Shine but a moment, it shall rise;
Let but the dew of thy soft hand
Refresh the stem, it straight shall stand:
Already, see, it swells, it grows,
Its head is redder than the rose,
Its shrivelled fruit, of dusky hue,
Now glows, a present fit for Sue:
The balm of life each artery fills,
And in o'erflowing drops distils.
Oh me! cried Susan, when is this?
What strange tumultuous throbs of bliss!
Sure, never mortal, till this hour,
Felt such emotion at a flower:

Oh, serpent! cunning to deceive,
Sure, 'tis this tree that tempted Eve;
The crimson apples hang so fair,
Alas! what woman could forbear?
Well, hast thou guessed, my love, I cried,
It is the tree by which she died;
The tree which could content her,
All nature, Susan, seeks the centre;
Yet, let us still, poor Eve forgive,
It's the tree by which we live;
For lovely woman still it grows,
And in the centre only blows.
But chief for thee, it spreads its charms,
For paradise is in thy arms. –
I ceased, for nature kindly here
Began to whisper in her ear:
And lovely Sue lay softly panting,
While the geranium tree was planting.
'Til in the heat of amorous strife,
She burst the mellow tree of life.
'Oh heaven!' cried Susan, with a sigh,
'The hour we taste – we surely die;
Strange raptures seize my fainting frame,
And all my body glows with flame;
Yet let me snatch one parting kiss
To tell my love I die with bliss:
That pleased, thy Susan yields her breath;
Oh! who would live if this be death!'

William Blake
1757–1827

'*In a wife*'

In a wife I would desire
What in whores is always found –
The lineaments of gratified desire.

from *Visions of the Daughters of Albion*

The moment of desire! the moment of desire! the virgin
That pines for man shall awaken her womb to enormous joys
In the secret shadows of her chamber: the youth shut up from
The lustful joy shall forget to generate & create an amorous image
In the shadows of his curtains and in the folds of his silent pillow.

from *Jerusalem* (*Plate 69*)

Embraces are Cominglings: from the Head even to the Feet;
And not a pompous High Priest entering by a Secret Place.

Robert Burns
1759–96

Gie The Lass Her Fairin'

O gie the lass her fairin' lad,   *food*
   O gie the lass her fairin',
An' something else she'll gie to you,
   That's waly worth the wearin';   *well worth*
Syne coup her o'er amang the creels,   *overturn*
   When ye hae taen your brandy,
The mair she bangs the less she squeels,
   An' hey for houghmagandie.   *fornication*

Then gie the lass a fairin', lad,
   O gie the lass her fairin',
And she'll gie you a hairy thing,
   An' of it be na sparin';
But coup her o'er amang the creels,
   An' bar the door wi' baith your heels,
The mair she bangs the less she squeels,
   An' hey for houghmagandie.

Nine Inch Will Please A Lady

'Come rede me, dame, come tell me, dame,   *advise*
  My dame come tell me truly,
What length o' graith, when weel ca'd hame,   *equipment*
  Will sair a woman duly?'   *serve*
The carlin clew her wanton tail,   *old woman, fondled*
  Her wanton tail sae ready –
'I learn'd a sang in Annandale,
  Nine inch will please a lady.

But for a koontrie cunt like mine,   *country*
  In sooth, we're nae sae gentle;
We'll tak tway thumb-bread to the nine,   *two thumbs' breadth*
  And that's a sonsy pintle: *lively penis*
O Leeze me on my Charlie lad,   *give thanks for*
  I'll ne'er forget my Charlie!
Tway roarin handfu's and a daud,   *lump*
  He nidge't it in fu' rarely.

But weary fa' the laithron doup,   *curses on, lazy rump*
  And may it ne'er be thrivin!
It's no the length that maks me loup,
  But it's the double drivin.
Come nidge me, Tam, come nudge me, Tam,
  Come nidge me o'er the nyvel!   *navel*
Come lowse and lug your battering ram,   *loosen, pull*
  And thrash him at my gyvel!'

My Girl, She's Airy

My Girl she's airy, she's buxom and gay,
Her breath is as sweet as the blossoms in May;
  A touch of her lips it ravishes quite;
She's always good natur'd, good humor'd and free;
She dances, she glances, she smiles with a glee;
  Her eyes are the lightnings of joy and delight;
Her slender neck, her handsome waist
Her hair well buckl'd, her stays well lac'd,

Her taper white leg, with an et, and a c,
    For her a b, e, d, and her c, u, n, t,
    And Oh, for the joys of a long winter night!!!

from **The Merry Muses of Caledonia**
18th century

Ellibanks

Ellibanks and Ellibraes,
    My blessin's ay befa' them,
Tho' I wish I had brunt a' my claes,   *burnt*
    The first time e'er I saw them:
Your succar kisses were sae sweet,   *sugar*
    Deil damn me gin I ken, man,   *if*
How ye gart me lay my legs aside,   *got me to*
    And lift my sark myself, man.   *shift*

There's no a lass in a' the land,
    Can fuck sae weel as I can;
Louse down your breeks, lug out your wand,   *loosen, pull*
    Hae ye nae mind to try, man:
For ye're the lad that wears the breeks,
    And I'm the lass that loes ye;
Deil rive my cunt to candle-wicks,   *tear*
    Gif ever I refuse ye!!!

I'll clasp my arms about your neck,
    As souple as an eel, jo;
I'll cleek my houghs about your arse,   *hook my thighs*
    As I were gaun to speel, jo;   *climb*
I'll cleek my houghs about your arse,
    As I were gaun to speel, jo;
And if Jock thief he should slip out,
    I'll ding him wi' my heel, jo.   *hit*

Green be the broom on Ellibraes,
　And yellow be the gowan!
My wame it fistles ay like flaes,　　　　*belly fidgets like flies*
　As I come o'er the knowe, man:
There I lay glowran to the moon,
　Your mettle wadna daunton,　　　　*awe*
For hard your hurdies hotch'd aboon,　　*buttocks jerked above*
　While I below lay panting.

Wad Ye Do That?

Gudewife, when your gudeman's frae hame,
　Might I but be sae bauld,
As come to your bed-chamber,
　When winter nights are cauld;
As come to your bed-chamber,
　When nights are cauld and wat,
And lie in your gudeman's stead,
　Wad ye do that?

Young man, an ye should be so kind,
　When our gudeman's frae hame,
As come to my bed-chamber,
　Where I am lain my lane;
And lie in our gudeman's stead,
　I will tell you what,
He fucks me five times ilka night,
　Wad ye do that?

John Anderson, My Jo

John Anderson, my jo, John,
　I wonder what ye mean,
To lie sae lang i' the mornin',
　And sit sae late at e'en?
Ye'll bleer a' your een, John,
　And why do ye so?
Come sooner to your bed at een,
　John Anderson, my jo.

John Anderson, my jo, John,
   When first that ye began,
Ye had as good a tail-tree,
   As ony ither man;
But now it's waxen wan, John,
   And wrinkles to and fro;
I've twa gae-ups for ae gae-down,
   John Anderson, my jo.

I'm backit like a salmon,
   I'm breastit like a swan;
My wame it is a down-cod,
   My middle ye may span:
Frae my tap-knot to my tae, John,
   I'm like the new-fa'n snow;
And it's a' for your convenience,
   John Anderson, my jo.

O it is a fine thing
   To keep out o'er the dyke;
But its a meikle finer thing,
   To see your hurdies fyke;   *buttocks move*
To see your hurdies fyke, John,
   And hit the rising blow;
It's then I like your chanter-pipe,
   John Anderson, my jo.

When ye come on before, John,
   See that ye do your best;
When ye begin to haud me,
   See that ye grip me fast;
See that ye grip me fast, John,
   Until that I cry 'Oh!'
Your back shall crack or I do that,
   John Anderson, my jo.

John Anderson, my jo, John,
   Ye're welcome when ye please;
It's either in the warm bed
   Or else aboon the claes: *above the covers*

Or ye shall hae the horns, John,
   Upon your head to grow;
An' that's the cuckold's mallison,   *curse*
   John Anderson, my jo.

Thomas Moore
1779–1852

An Argument

I've oft been told by learned friars,
   That wishing and the crime are one,
And Heaven punishes desires
   As much as if the deed were done.

If wishing damns us, you and I
   Are damn'd to all our heart's content;
Come, then, at least we may enjoy
   Some pleasure for our punishment!

George Gordon, Lord Byron
1788–1824

from *Don Juan* (Canto II, clxxxvi)

A long, long kiss, a kiss of youth, and love,
   And beauty, all concentrating like rays
Into one focus, kindled from above;
   Such kisses as belong to early days,
Where heart, and soul, and sense, in concert move,
   And the blood's lava, and the pulse a blaze,
Each kiss a heart-quake, – for a kiss's strength,
I think it must be reckoned by its length.

Heinrich Heine

1797–1856

The Song of Songs

Woman's white body is a song,
    And God Himself's the author;
In the eternal book of life
    He put the lines together.

It was a thrilling hour; the Lord
    Felt suddenly inspired;
Within his brain the stubborn stuff
    Was mastered, fused, and fired.

Truly, the Song of Songs is this,
    The greatest of his trophies:
This living poem where soft limbs
    Are a rare pair of strophes.

Oh, what a heavenly masterpiece
    That neck and its relation
To the fair head, like an idea
    Crowned with imagination.

In pointed epigrams, the breasts
    Rise under teasing rallies;
And a caesura lies between
    The loveliest of valleys.

He published the sweet parallel
    Of thighs – what joy to be there!
The fig-leaf grotto joining them
    Is not a bad place either.

It is no cold, conceptual verse,
    No patterned abstract study!
This poem sings with rhyming lips,
    With sweet bones and warm body.

Here breathes the deepest poetry!
    Beauty in every motion!
Upon its brow it bears the stamp
    Of His complete devotion.

Here in the dust, I praise Thee, Lord.
   We are – and well I know it –
Rank amateurs, compared to Thee:
   Heaven's first major poet!

I'll dedicate myself to learn
   This song, the lyric body;
With ardour and with energy
   All day – and night – I'll study!

Yes, day and night, I'll never lack
   For constant application;
And though the task may break my back
   I'll ask for no vacation!

Alfred, Lord Tennyson
1809–92

from *Merlin and Vivien*

A twist of gold was round her hair; a robe
Of samite without price, that more expressed
Than hid her, clung about her lissome limbs,
In colour like the satin-shining palm
On sallows in the windy gleams of March:

* * *

And lissome Vivien, holding by his heel,
Writhed towards him, slided up his knee and sat,
Behind his ankle twined her hollow feet
Together, curved an arm about his neck,
Clung, like a snake.

Walt Whitman

1819–92

from *I Sing The Body Electric* (part 5)

This is the female form,
A divine nimbus exhales from it from head to foot,
It attracts with fierce undeniable attraction,
I am drawn by its breath as if I were no more than a helpless
    vapour, all falls aside but myself and it,
Books, art, religion, time, the visible and solid earth, and what was
    expected of heaven or feared of hell, are now consumed,
Mad filaments, ungovernable shoots play out of it, the response
    likewise ungovernable,
Hair, bosom, hips, bend of legs, negligent falling hands all diffused,
    mine too diffused,
Ebb stung by the flow and flow stung by the ebb, love-flesh swelling
    and deliciously aching,
Limitless limpid jets of love hot and enormous, quivering jelly of
    love, white-blow and delirious juice,
Bridegroom night of love working surely and softly into the prostrate
    dawn,
Undulating into the willing and yielding day,
Lost in the cleave of the clasping and sweet-fleshed day.

This is the nucleus – after the child is born of woman, man is born of
    woman,
This is the bath of birth, this the merge of small and large, and the
    outlet again.

Be not ashamed women, your privilege encloses the rest, and is the
    exit of the rest,
You are the gates of the body, and you are the gates of the soul.

The female contains all qualities and tempers them,
She is in her place and moves with perfect balance,
She is all things duly veiled, she is both passive and active,

She is to conceive daughters as well as sons, and sons as well as
   daughters.
As I see my soul reflected in Nature,
As I see through a mist, One with inexpressible completeness,
   sanity, beauty,
See the bent head and arms folded over the breast, the Female I see.

from *A Woman Waits for Me*

A woman waits for me, she contains all, nothing is lacking,
Yet all were lacking if sex were lacking, or if the moisture of the right
   man were lacking.

Sex contains all, bodies, souls,
Meanings, proofs, purities, delicacies, results, promulgations,
Songs, commands, health, pride, the maternal mystery, the seminal
   milk,
All hopes, benefactions, bestowals, all the passions, loves, beauties,
   delights of the earth,
All the governments, judges, gods, followed persons of the earth,
These are contained in sex as parts of itself and justifications of itself.
Without shame the man I like knows and avows the deliciousness of
   his sex,
Without shame the woman I like knows and avows hers.

Now I will dismiss myself from impassive women,
I will go stay with her who waits for me, and with those women that
   are warm-blooded and sufficient for me,
I see that they understand me and do not deny me,
I see that they are worthy of me, I will be the robust husband of
   those women.

Charles Baudelaire

1821–67

The Jewels

The treasure was naked and, knowing my heart,
Had kept her sonorous jewels on when undressed;
Their haughty splendour made her look the part
Proud Moorish slavegirls play when happiest.

When its bright, mocking noise dances on air
This shimmering world of metal and stone
Puts me in ecstasy, and I adore
These objects in which sound and light combine.

So she lay back and let herself be loved
And, high on the divan, she smiled as if
My love, deep and gentle as the sea, moved
Towards her as the waves towards a cliff.

She transfixed my eyes like a tamed tigress,
Vaguely dreamily she tried out poses,
And her frankness combined with her lewdness
Gave new charm to her metamorphoses.

And so her arms her loins her legs her thighs
Gliding like oil and curving like a swan
Swam before my calm all-seeing eyes;
And her breasts and belly, grapes of my vine,

Advanced, more tempting than evil angels,
To disturb my soul's serenity,
Knocking it down from the rock of crystals
Where it had settled calm and solitary.

I thought I saw a new design unite
Antiope's hips and torso of a boy –
Her waist above her hips appeared so slight.
On that wild dark skin rouge was a sheer joy.

– And as the lamp resigned itself to die,
As the fire alone shed light on the room
Each time it flickered with a fiery sigh
It gave that amber skin a blood-red bloom.

Spleen

Come to my heart you cruel indifferent soul,
Adorable tigress, contented bitch;
I want my hands to settle in the rich
Abundance of your locks of hair awhile;

In underskirts uplifted with your scent
Smooth and smother my exhausted head,
Inhale, as from a withered flowerbed,
The musky aftermath of passion spent.

I want to sleep! to sleep more than to live!
In a deep slumber delicious as death
I'll regulate my kissing with my breath
And burnish up your copper skin with love.

Nothing compares with your bed's abyss
When it comes to soaking up my tears;
Omnipotent oblivion appears
On your lips and Lethe flows in each kiss.

My fate, from now on, will be my delight,
I will embrace it like a faithful friend;
A docile martyr, wrongfully condemned,
Whose fervour keeps the rising flames alight,

I shall extract, to mitigate my hurt,
Soothing drinks and satisfying tastes
From the stiff nipples of those gorgeous breasts
That never could point inwards to a heart.

To She Who Is Too Gay

Your head, gesture and atmosphere
Are lovely as a country place;
Laughter flits about your face
Like a fresh wind in cloudless air.

The dull onlooker you brush past
Is startled by the healthy glow
Shimmering above the shadow
That your arms and shoulders cast.

The vibrant colours that entrance
And titivate the clothes you wear
Suggest to poets everywhere
The image of a floral dance.

These daring dresses indicate
The pattern of your cunning brain;
So, crazy for you, I complain
My passion mixes love with hate.

If, in a garden, I should rest
My temperamental indolence,
Like an ironical presence
The sunshine gets beneath my breast;

And if the spring's green arrogance
Burdens my heart with guilt and shame
I'll kill a flower, and put the blame
On nature's sheer impertinence.

Thus I would want to come one night,
When the sensual hour is due,
Towards the treasury of you,
Like a coward in the quiet,

To chastise your ecstatic flesh,
To bruise your bosom's innocence,
And open in you an immense
Infinitely shocking gash,

And – my heartbeat getting faster –
Through these freshly opened lips,
More beautiful, more brilliant shapes,
To inject my venom, sister.

Dante Gabriel Rossetti
1828–82

from *Jenny*

Why, Jenny, as I watch you there –
For all your wealth of loosened hair,
Your silk ungirdled and unlaced
And warm sweets open to the waist,
All golden in the lamplight's gleam –
You know not what a book you seem,
Half-read by lightning in a dream!

The Kiss (Sonnet IV)

What smouldering senses in death's sick delay
   Or seizure of malign vicissitude
   Can rob this body of honour, or denude
This soul of wedding-raiment worn today?
For lo! even now my lady's lips did play
   With these my lips such consonant interlude
   As laurelled Orpheus longed for when he wooed
The half-drawn hungering face with that last lay.

I was a child beneath her touch, – a man
When breast to breast we clung, even I and she –
   A spirit when her spirit looked through me –
A god when all our life-breath met to fan
Our life-blood, till love's emulous ardours ran,
   Fire within fire, desire in deity.

Algernon Charles Swinburne
1837–1909

Love and Sleep

Lying asleep between the strokes of night
 I saw my love lean over my sad bed,
 Pale as the duskiest lily's leaf or head,
Smooth-skinned and dark, with bare throat made to bite,
Too wan for blushing and too warm for white,
 But perfect-coloured without white or red.
 And her lips opened amorously, and said –
I wist not what, saving one word – Delight.

And all her face was honey to my mouth,
 And all her body pasture to mine eyes;
  The long lithe arms and hotter hands than fire,
The quivering flanks, hair smelling of the south,
 The bright light feet, the splendid supple thighs
  And glittering eyelids of my soul's desire.

Paul Verlaine
1844–96

Openers

I want to get away into your thighs and cheeks,
You whores, true priests, sole agents of the one true God's,
Whether you've taken vows, are moderns or antiques:
I'll live in your pink cloisters and your honeyed squads.

Your marvellous feet, that only take you out to get
A lover, only bring you back for lovers, rest
Only in bed at lovetime till they smoothly pet
The lover's feet as he lies panting on the nest –

Your feet, so squeezed and sniffed and kissed and licked, from soles
To toes, each toe mouth-organed, and then ankles too,
With their slow veins that snake in coils towards their holes,
Lovelier than saints' or heroes' feet, and what they do.

And how I love your mouth: its games so full of grace
They make the lips begin to seek, the tongue to hide,
The teeth to nibble tongue, or something in its place –
Such tricks are almost better than it is inside.

And then your breasts, the double mount of pride and lust:
Between them my male pride sometimes goes chimneying
And swelling rubs there like a wild boar in the dust
On Mount Parnassus till its head begins to sing.

Your arms, so fine, so pale, excite my reverence:
Tender and hard, and sinewy at need, but plump
And warm in love, though after chilled as monuments,
So pale, so fine, they stir my senses like your rump.

My admiration wanders down those arms to hands:
Hands that from lazing and caressing are so fair,
Hands that revive our numb and softly shrinking glands
And wag them with an infinitely worried care.

Well, all that beauty's nothing, whores, compared with your
Arses and cunts which give the feel of Paradise –
We know we'll go there by this haze of sensual awe –
Holies of Holies, Arks of Covenants of vice.

And that is why, my Sisters, to your thighs and cheeks
I want to get away, true friends to lecherous sods
Whether you've taken vows, are moderns or antiques:
I'll live in your pink cloisters and your honeyed quads.

Foursome

Where the waist falls, where childhood's dream of being good
    Falls to the buttocks, throne of our disgrace,
Where fleshly beauty triumphs more than in the face,
Buttocks, where white and round form a Beautitude!

Breasts, double mount of blue and milk with two brown crests
   Commanding views of dale and sacred wood,
Breasts, whose delightful tips like living fruit are food
To tongue and mouth drunk on these coupled fortunes, breasts!

Buttocks, their delicate gully full of dark pine shade
   Where lust prowls madly down the downy trail,
Dear pillows, cushion deeply creased for nose or tail,
A cool place to rest hands when all their tricks are played!

Breasts, to the hands they fill a feast of delicate size,
   Breasts heavy, strong, proud and contemptuous,
Cradled and rocked, feeling they've won, looking at us
And our prostrations from the corners of their eyes!

Buttocks, big sisters of the breasts, more natural
   And open, parted in a candid smile,
So simple they don't care to bully or beguile,
All their dictatorship just being beautiful.

Here I invoke you four: tyrants, but sweet and just,
   The imperial pair, the princely underlings,
That bend the vulgar and admit anointed kings,
Hosannah, Rumpus Rex and Venerable Bust!

Troilets for a Virtue in Excuse for Mine Being Small

Great length and breadth in what you feel
Is different from how deep it goes.
I wouldn't claim for my appeal
Great length and breadth in what you feel.
Come kindly though, and clinch my deal
Where – between flesh and blood – it rose.
Great length and breadth in what you feel
Is different from how deep it goes.

For quality is best, they say,
However large the quantity.
The glutton yields to the gourmet,
For quality is best, they say.

Be nice: come, let your taste betray
To my desire that they agree.
For quality is best, they say,
However large the quantity.

Small fish get big as they can be
If Someone lends them Life enough.
Oh, be that Someone: guarantee
Small fish get big as big can be.
I'll pay you back what you lend me:
That joyful enviable stuff!
Small fish get big as big can be
If Someone lends them Life enough.

This point pokes fun at all your pride,
Standing up proud and stout of heart.
Give in: be on the yielding side.
This point pokes fun at all your pride
As at that pussy that's one-eyed,
And dooms you to the outraged part.
This point pokes fun at all your pride,
Standing up proud and stout of heart.

Notwithstanding, the time soon comes:
It's done. Well watered. Order reigns.
With drawn sword and a tuck of drums,
Not with standing, the time soon comes.
Now joy and virtue do their sums:
My point weeps; pride bleeds; who complains?
Not withstanding, the time soon comes:
It's done. Well watered. Order reigns.

Anointed Vessel

Admire the watered silky gap,
Mahomet's paradise, that shows
My creamy entry through the lap
Of luxuries that once were rose.

179

Oh, tired old eyes, take up delight
As painters do, forget your tears
Though warranted, in this rich sight –
This vessel that uplifts and cheers:

In a soft box of plushy fluff,
Black, but with glints of copper-red
And edges crinkly like a ruff,
Lies the great god of gems in bed,

Throbbing with sap and life, and sends
In wafts the best news ever sent,
A perfume his ecstatic friends
Think stolen from each element.

But contemplate this temple, cont-
emplate, then get your breath, and kiss
The jewel having fits in front,
The ruby grinning for its bliss,

Flower of the inner court, kid brother
So mad about the taller one
It kisses till they both half-smother
And puff, then pulse, in unison . . .

But rest; you're blazing now; relax.
It too should calm and cool; but rest?
In those embrasures and hot cracks
Of thigh and belly, breast and breast?

No, soon its swaying tipsiness
Wins my parts over to a man.
My flesh stands up and nods: right dress!
Begin again where we began!

Low Scene

The apprentice – fifteen, ugly, not too thin,
Nice in a softish uncouth way, dull skin,
Bright deepset eyes – blue overalls – pulls out
His springy, stiff, well-tuned, quite man-sized spout

And rams the boss's wife – big but still good,
Flopped on the bed's edge – what an attitude! –
Legs up, breasts out, one hand parting her placket.
To see him crush her arse under his jacket
And quickstep forward more than back, it's clear
He's not afraid how deep he plants his gear
Or if the lady fruits – she doesn't care –
Isn't her trusty cuckold always there? –
So when she reaches, as he shoots his goal,
That rapture of the body as a whole,
She cries, 'You've made a child, I feel it, love,
And love you more,' and after his last shove
Adds, 'Look, the christening sweets,' and squats and tries
To heft and kiss his bollocks through his flies.

A Brief Moral

A golden head, head of a fainting grace;
Below a throat that purrs, outstanding paps
With dark medallions and stiff glowing caps –
This bust disposed in a low, cushioned place;
While in between two legs that lift and beat,
A woman on her knees – Love only knows
What service she attends – to heaven shows
The artless epic of her shining seat,
Beauty's clear mirror, where she loves to gaze,
See and believe herself. O woman's arse,
Roundly defeating man's in every class,
O arse of arses: Glory! Worship! Praise!

Anonymous
19th century

The Origin of Species

When Adam and Eve were first put into Eden,
They never once thought of that pleasant thing – breeding
Though they had not a rag to cover their front,
Adam sported his prick, and Eve sported her cunt.
                              Derry down.

Adam's prick was so thick and so long – such a teaser;
Eve's cunt was so hairy and fat – such a breezer;
Adam's thing was just formed any maiden to please,
And his bollocks hung down very near to his knees.
                              Derry down.

Eve played with his balls, and thought it no harm:
He fingered her quim and ne'er felt alarm;
He tickled her bubbies, she rubbed up his yarp,
And yet for a fuck, why they felt no regard.
                              Derry down.

But when Mrs Eve did taste of the fruit,
It was then that her eyes first beheld Adam's root;
Then he ate an apple, and after he had done't,
Why then he first found out the value of cunt.
                              Derry down.

Then they sat they made fig leaves, that's fiddle-de-dee.
He wanted a quim, and quite ready was she;
They gazed on their privates with mutual delight,
And she soon found a hole to put jock out of sight!
                              Derry down.

Then Adam soon laid Mrs Eve on the grass,
He popped in his prick, she heaved up her arse;
He wriggled, she wiggled, they both stuck to one tether
And she tickled his balls, till they both came together!
                              Derry down.

Since then, all her children are filled with desire,
And the women a stiff standing prick all require!
And no son of Adam will e'er take affront,
For where is the man that can live without cunt?

Derry down.

The Meeting of the Waters
(*A Parody on Moore's Melody*)

There is not in this wide world a valley so sweet,
As that vale where the thighs of a pretty girl meet:
Oh, the last ray of feeling and life must depart,
Ere the bloom of that valley shall fade from my heart.

Yet it is not that nature has shed o'er the scene,
The purest of red, the most delicate skin,
'Tis not the sweet smell of the genial hill;
Ah, no! it is something more exquisite still.

'Tis because the last favours of woman are there,
Which make every part of her body more dear.
We feel how the charms of Nature improve,
When we bathe in the spendings of her whom we love.

Sweet valley of Venus, how calm could I rest,
Deep, deep, within thee, on the girl I love best;
When the throbs of fierce passion in ecstasy cease,
And our hearts, like thy waters, are mingled in peace.

Cunt

Cunt is a greedy, unsatisfied glutton.
All women are ready to yield up their mutton;
Finger them, fuck them, and do as you please
They have such an itching, you never can teaze;
Thrust in your penis from morning till night,
Still they are ready to come with delight;
Of bollox and all you could give them galore,
By God! They're so greedy, they still cry for more.

Fuck till your penis no longer will stand,
She still your bollox will teaze with her hand;
Rub it and dandle it over again
Still she will have it, though writhing with pain;
Let it be long, or let it be thick,
Women are never contented with prick:
And when all their power and vigour are past,
With prick in their hand, they will breathe out their last.

The Reverie

What dull and senseless lumps we'd be,
If never of felicity
We tasted; and what bliss is there
To equal that of fucking rare?
An age of grief, an age of pain,
I would endure and ne'er complain;
To purchase but an hour's charms
While wriggling in a maiden's arms!
And hugging her to heavenly rest;
My hand reposing on her breast!
Her arse my own, her thighs my screen,
My penis standing in between!
My bollox hanging down below,
And banging 'gainst her arse of snow;
Or else grasped firmly in her hand,
To make my yard more stiffly stand.
How soon the blood glows in the veins,
And nature all its power now strains;
The belly heaves, the penis burns,
The maiden all its heat returns,
'Till passion holds triumphant sway,
And both the lovers die away.

Origin of Copulation

Success to dame Nature, for 'twas by her plan,
That woman first thought of enjoyment from man;
She knew that of pleasure they'd never be sick,
And so out of kindness, invented a prick!
 A stiff standing, glorious prick!
 Voluptuous, rubicund prick!
Oh, surely, of fortune it came in the nick,
Good natured dame Nature to give us a prick!

Without it how lost would a poor maiden be,
It tickles her quim, makes her water run free;
Most women a handle would have to their front,
So they've only to thrust a long prick in their cunt!
 Their hairy, voluptuous cunt!
 Their sweet little, queer little cunt!
What damsel no handle would have to their front?
And prick e'er has been a great friend unto cunt!

When nature to women gave two mouths, she willed
Of course, that they both should be equally filled,
And if women will look after one mouth, you know
That prick will look after the mouth that's below!
 Stiff standing, glorious prick!
 Voluptuous, rubicund prick!
Oh, surely, of fortune it came in the nick,
Good natured dame Nature to give us a prick!

When sorrow torments lovely woman, oh dear,
A mighty good fucking will banish despair;
If her belly but aches, why we all know the trick,
There's nothing can ease it so well as a prick!
 A nice luscious prick!
 A stiff standing prick!
For any young maiden it can do the trick,
Oh, joys there are plenty, but nothing like prick!

Taking a Maidenhead
(Air – '*Gee, ho Dobbin*')

Oh, Maidenhead taking's a very great bore,
It makes cunt and prick so confoundedly sore;
But fucking the third time's like heaven above,
For your prick then glides in, as you draw on a glove!
  Gee up, Roger,
  Wag up, Roger,
  Roger's a thing that all women admire!

Oh, give me a damsel of blooming fifteen,
With two luscious thighs and a mouse-trap between,
With the fringe on the edge and two red lips I say,
In her cunt I'd be diving by night and by day!
  Gee up, &c.

That woman would be a disgrace to our land,
Who would not take a prick, when it stiffly does stand;
And when it droops low as if it were in dread,
She must tickle the balls till it lifts up its head!
  Gee up, &c.

Cunt is a treasure which monarchs admire,
Cunt is a thing that my theme doth inspire;
Cunt is a mighty temptation to sin,
But cunt is a hole that I'd never be in!
  Gee up, &c.

Prick is its friend, its first cousin, I ween,
Tho' prick I confess is a rare go-between;
Prick to a woman much joy can impart,
And prick is a thing that she loves in her heart!
  Gee up, &c.

Then here's to the female who yields to a man,
And here's to the man who'll fuck when he can,
For fucking creates all our joy upon earth,
And from fucking you know, we all date our birth.
  Gee up, &c.

Facetiae

Cease, foolish painters, Hercules to draw
With wooden club, inspiring man with awe;
A different club that here should adorn,
This god's most powerful weapon is the horn;
No mightier spear than that the champion hurls,
With which one night he fucked three score of girls!
A crowd of grave enquirers made resort,
To where the learned doctors held their court;
And asked them who had been that serpent brute
Which tempted mother Eve to eat the fruit?
'Ye silly men,' the sages did reply,
'Why do you waste your time and ours, oh, why?
Eve's tempting snake was but a long and thick,
Great, knotty, ruddy, massy, mighty prick!'

The Pitman's Lovesong

Aw wish my lover she was a cherry
Growing upon yon cherry tree,
And aw mysel a bonny blackbird;
How aw would peck that cherry cherree.

Aw wish my lover she was a red rose
Growing upon yon garden wa',
And aw mysel was a butterflee;
O on that red rosie aw wad fa'.

Aw wish my lover she was a fish
Sooming doon in the saut sea,
And aw mysel was a fisher lad;
O aw wad catch her reet cunningly.

Aw wish my love was in a kist
And aw mysel to carry the key.
Then aw wad gan tin her when aw had list,
And bear my hinny good company.

Aw wish my love she was a grey ewe
Grazing by yonder river side,
And aw myself a bonny black tup;
O on that ewie how aw wad ride.

O she's bonny, she wondrous canny,
O she's well far'd to see,
For the mair aw think on my love's on upon her,
And under her apron fain wad aw be.

Aw wish my lover she was a bee skep,
And aw mysel a bumble bee,
That aw might be a lodger within her;
She's sweeter than honey or honeycombe tea.

Aw wish my lover was a ripe turd,
Smoking doon in yon dyke side,
And aw myself was a shitten flee;
Aw'd sook her all up before she was dried.

O my hinny, my bonny hinny,
O my hinny, my bonny hinnee;
The mair aw think on her, my heart's set upon her.
She's fairer than ever she used to be.

Long Peggin' Awl

As I was a-walking one morning in May,
I met a pretty fair maid, her gown it was gay.
I stepped up to her and back she did fall.
She wanted to be played with the long peggin' awl.

I said 'Pretty fair maid, will you travel with me
Unto foreign countries strange things for to see?
And I will protect you whate'er may befall,
And follow your love with his long peggin' awl.'

Then home to her parents she went straightway,
And unto her mother these words she did say:
'I'll follow my true love, whate'er may befall,
I'll follow my love with his long peggin' awl.'

'O daughter, O daughter, how can you say so?
For young men are false, you very well know.
They'll tell you fine things and the devil and all,
And leave you big-bellied with the long peggin' awl.'

'O mother, O mother, now do not say so,
Before you were sixteen you very well know,
There was father and mother and baby and all.
You followed my dad for his long peggin' awl.'

The Thrashing Machine

For there was an old farmer in Down he did dwell,
He'd one pretty servant, her name it was Nell.
He'd one pretty servant she was scarce seventeen,
And he showed her the works of his thrashing machine.

Says Nell to the farmer, 'It's a fine summer's day,
While the rest of the farmers are off making hay,
Come into the barn where we won't be seen,
And the two of us start working our thrashing machine.'

Oh, Nell she stepped forward and into the house.
The boss got the harness and strapped her right on.
Nell took the handle and turned on the steam,
And the two of them start working their thrashing machine.

Oh, six months being over and nine coming on,
Nell's skirt wouldn't meet nor her drawers wouldn't go on;
It's under her oxter like a young fairy queen.
I will have you transported for your thrashing machine.

Oh, up comes the Judge with a pen in his claw,
He says, 'Lovely Nell, you have broken the law;'
'No, sir,' says she, 'it's plain to be seen,
I needed the strength of his thrashing machine.'

The Cuckoo's Nest

There is a thorn bush in oor kail-yard,
There is a thorn bush in oor kail-yard,
At the back of thorn bush there stands a lad and lass
But they're busy, busy hairin' at the cuckoo's nest.

It is thorned, it is sprinkled, it is compassed all around,
It is thorned, it is sprinkled and it isn't easy found.
She said, 'Young man, you're blundering. I said it was nae true.'
But I left her with the makin's o' a young cuckoo.

It's hi the cuckin, ho the cuckin, hi the cuckoo's nest,
It's hi the cuckin, ho the cuckin, hi the cuckoo's nest.
I'll gie onybody a shilling and a bottle o' the best
If they'll rumple up the feathers o' the cuckoo's nest.

Cruising Round Yarmouth

While cruisin' round Yarmouth one day for a spree,
I met a fair damsel, the wind blowing free.
'I'm a fast going clipper, my kind sir,' said she,
'I'm ready for cargo, my hold it is free.'
    Singing *fal-the-ral-laddy*, *right-fal-the-ral-day*,
    Fal-the-ral-laddy, *right-fal-the-ral-day*.

I gave her the rope and I took her in tow.
From yardarm to yardarm a-towing we go.
I lift up her hatches, found plenty of room,
And into her cabin I stuck my jibboom.

She took me upstairs and her topsails she lowered,
In a neat little parlour she soon had me moored,
She laid in her foresails, her staysails an' all,
With her lily-white hand on my reef-tackle fall.

I said, 'Pretty fair maid, it's time to give o'er,
Betwixt wind and water you've ran me ashore.
My shot locker's empty and powders all spent.
I can't fire a shot for it's choked at the vent.'

Here's luck to the girl with the black curly locks.
Here's luck to the girl who ran Jack on the rocks.
Here's luck to the doctor who eased all his pain;
He squared his mainyards; he's a-cruisin' again.

Blow the Candle Out

There was a young apprentice who went to meet his dear,
The moon was shinin' brightly and the stars were viewin' clear.
He went to his love's window and he called her by her name,
Then soon she rose and let him in, went back to bed again.

Saying: 'Willie, dearest Willie, tonight will be your doom.
Strip off into your nightshirt and bear one night within.
The streets they are too lonely for you to walk about,
So come roll me in your arms, love, and we'll blow the candle out.

My father and my mother, next bedroom they do lie,
Kissing and embracing, and why not you and I?
Kissing and embracing without a fear or doubt,
So come roll me in your arms, love, and we'll blow the candle out.'

It was six months and after six, six months ago today,
He wrote to me a letter saying he was far away;
He wrote to me a letter without a fear or doubt,
And he never said when he'd come back to blow the candle out.

Come all you gallant highway girls pay heed to what I say,
Never court a young man that ploughs the angry sea;
For some day or another when walking out about,
He will do to you as he done to me when he blew the candle out.

Never Wed An Old Man

For an aul' man come courtin' me,
  Hi-doo-a-darrity,
An aul' man come courtin' me,
  Hi-doo-a-day.
For an aul' man come courtin' me,
  Hi-doo-a-darrity,
Maids, when you're young never wed a aul' man.

For when we went to the church
I left him in the lurch,
When we went to the church,
Me being young;
When we went to the church
I left him in the lurch,
Maids, when you're young never wed a aul' man.

For when we went to oor tea
He started teasing me,
When we went to oor tea,
Me being young;
When we went to oor tea
He started teasing me,
Maids, when you're young never wed a aul' man.

When we went to oor bed
He lay as he was dead,
When we went to oor bed,
Me being young;
When we went to oor bed
He lay as he was dead,
Maids, when you're young never wed a aul' man.

For he has no tooralo,
Right-fol-the-dooralo,
He has no tooralo
Right-fol-the-day;
For he has no tooralo
To fill up my dooralo,
Maids, when you're young never wed a aul' man.

Gabriele D'Annunzio
1863–1938

Silvered

When, half upraised, her belly to the sand,
Naked she welcomes the slow-conquering tide,
Then, in the full moon's radiance, she appears
Like some great silver statue lying there.

A Callipygian Venus, lewdly posed –
Into the rounded surface of her sides
Two hollows sculpted, and her powerful spine
Furrowing deeply as she arches back.

The rising tide steals up and moistens her.
She starts and shudders at its icy touch,
Her loins a-tremble in their ecstasy.

The billows dash against her face, but still
She holds her chosen posture fearlessly
Till, at its height, the tide submerges her.

Bronzed

After her bathe, all dripping-wet, and swathed
In her dark hair, her body shivering,
She prints in the dry surface of the sand
The splendid contours of her flawless limbs.

Sometimes she grasps her bosom's living fruits
Causing their sturdy points to burgeon forth;
Sometimes she rolls about, and the coarse sand
Marks her smooth skin with curious designs.

Then, patterned thus, she offers up her all
To the moon's kiss, on seaweed-couch outspread,
Remaining motionless with skyward breast.

And from the distance on the background dark,
She looks like a great brazen statue, part-
Corroded by the sea's acidity.

from *The Fresh-Water Venus*

Agile and unabashed, she clambered down
Towards the river, like a parching hind.
The forest thrilled with tenderness for her.
The utmost reassurance filled her eyes;
And of such tawny blondness was her hair
That verily the bees must have been drawn,
As though towards some honey of their own,
By the deceptive lure of locks like those.

Reaching the edge, she paused reluctantly.
But soon those tresses worth the ancient comb
Of Cypris[37] had been knotted at her nape,
And, with no hint of modesty, she gave
To sun and water all her naked charms,
Entering navel-deep into the gulf
And glistening there just as Praxiteles
Had sculpted her at Cnidus and at Cos.[38]

O dream of beauty neath unhampered skies,
Dream by my earliest puberty conceived,
When I imagined, during studious nights,
The laurels of Ilissus[39] rising from
The lifeless pages to adorn my brow,
With Acidalian[40] roses twined – O dream,
You radiant bloomed at last without a veil,
Fulfilled in flesh beneath unhampered skies.

I peered between the grass. She stretched her arms
Towards a branch that, rich in clustered leaves,
Reached over her, and drew to it her form
Entire that flexed in undulations lithe.

Then, with a sudden spring, she straightened out
And swung herself to where the tide ran deep;
And there the water into turmoil stirred,
Foam-fertile neath the impact of her limbs.

Those lissom nudities that slipped into
The river bottom's mystery passed through
A spread of floating leaves that marked their course;
And close upon that course my own desire,
Thirsting to taste the flesh's ecstasies,
Followed with swiftly beating wings, as might
A vulture plunging from the loftiest heavens
Towards the odour of his carnal prey.

But when she smoothly laid her spotless frame
Across the water's lap, and so displayed
The scarlet berries of her upturned breasts,
While in her belly's flesh the navel shone
As if the seal of treasure there intact,
On the plump pubis and the hollowed groin
The clinging droplets in the curly fleece
Glittered like dew in some resplendent fern.

W. B. Yeats
1865–1939

The Lover's Song

Bird sighs for the air,
Thought for I know not where,
For the womb the seed sighs.
Now sinks the same rest
On mind, on nest,
On straining thighs.

Rubén Darío

1867–1916

'*Antonio, that good fellow*'

Antonio, that good fellow,
has recently got married
and is happy with his wife,
for there is no one lovelier,
sweeter, and more faithful,
more filled with affection,
more free of duplicity,
gentler of character,
easier to seduce –

Guillaume Apollinaire

1880–1918

The Skirt

Hello Germaine that's a fine skirt you have
A fine skirt for a queen A cruel queen
Let's feel the silk of it Silk from Japan
And trimmed with wide lace made on no machine

Your skirt's a silken bell whose double clapper
Your legs have struck the passing of my fancies
O Germaine now I ring it my breast heaving
My hands press down upon your willing haunches

Your bedroom O my bell is a fine belfry
My hands touch silk and seem to tear my ears
Those pegs are gallows on which skirts are hanging
Those hanging men are dazzling my eyes

Motionless as an owl the oil lamp watches

Gottfried Benn
1886–1956

Nightcafé IV

It's hardly worth the candle. Then – one pushes in
and tumbles: forth to the hem of the Lord's kingdom;
you love me, don't you? I was so lonesome.

The Blue Danube Waltz makes the sow emotional.
Her lips moan with it in three-four time. Downstream now
in the charming valley! There she sits with the lute and all.

The waiter rows about with slumber punches.
He swims to freedom. Flesh-foliage and whore-cheered autumns,
a flabby slide. Fat furrows. Hollows gutter;
the flesh is fluid; pour it as you will
about you:
                a slot full of screams our mouth.

Federico Garcia Lorca
1889–1936

The Unfaithful Wife

So I took her to the riverside
taking her for a virgin
but she had taken a husband.
Midsummer night, the Feast of St James:
it was a point of honour.
The streetlamps went off
and the crickets went on.
On the outskirts
I touched her sleeping breasts
and instantly they blossomed
like sprays of hyacinth.
The starch in her underskirt

grated on my ears like
a sheet of silk
lacerated by ten knives.
Without silver glinting on their leaves
the trees looked massive.
A horizon of dogs
Howls in the distance.

    Past the blackberries,
the rushes, the hawthorn,
under her hair in the sand
I made a hollow for her head.
I took off my tie,
she took off her dress.
I removed my gunbelt,
she removed her underwear.
Neither petals nor shells
match such delicate skin,
nor do moonlit mirrors
glow with such shine.
Her thighs struggled
like astonished fish
caught in a torrent
now fiery, now frozen.
That night I rode
on the best of roads,
my mother-of-pearl mount
free and unbridled.
As a man I hesitate to say
the things she said to me:
the seeds of understanding
breed discretion.
Covered in kisses and sand
I removed her from the riverside.
The swords of the lillies
cut through the atmosphere.

    I acted like the man I am,
a decent gypsy.
I gave her a big sewing-basket

of straw-coloured satin,
and preferred not to fall in love
because she had taken a husband
yet told me she was a virgin
when I took her by the riverside.

Hugh MacDiarmid
1892–1978

from *A Drunk Man Looks at the Thistle*

O wha's the bride that cairries the bunch
O' thistles blinterin' white?
Her cuckold bridegroom little dreids
What he sall ken this nicht.

For closer than gudeman can come
And closer to'r than hersel',
Wha didna need her maidenheid
Has wrocht his purpose fell.

O wha's been here afore me, lass,
And hoo did he get in?
– *A man that deed or I was born*
This evil thing has din.

And left, as it were on a corpse,
Your maidenheid to me?
– *Nae lass, gudeman, sin' Time began*
'S hed ony mair to gi'e.

But I can gi'e ye kindness, lad,
And a pair o' willin' hands,
And you sall ha'e my briests like stars,
My limbs like willow wands,

And on my lips ye'll heed nae mair,
And in my hair forget,
The seed o' a' the men that in
My virgin womb ha'e met . . .

from *Ode to All Rebels*

O she was fu' o' lovin' fuss
When I cut my hand and the bluid gushed oot
And cleverly she dressed the wound
And row'd it in a clout.   *wrapped, cloth*

O tenderly she tended me
But deep in her een I saw
The secret joy that men are whiles   *sometimes*
Obliged to bleed ana'.   *also*

I thanked her kindly and never let on,
Seein' she couldna understand,
That she wished me a wound faur waur to staunch   *far worse*
– And no' i' the hand!

e. e. cummings
1894–1962

'*she being Brand*'

she being Brand

-new; and you
know consequently a
little stiff i was
careful of her and (having

thoroughly oiled the universal
joint tested my gas felt of
her radiator made sure her springs were O.

K.) i went right to it flooded-the-carburettor cranked her

up, slipped the
clutch (and then somehow got into reverse she
kicked what
the hell) next
minute i was back in neutral tried and

again slo-wly; bare,ly nudg. ing (my

lev-er Right-
oh and her gears being in
Al shape passed
from low through
second-in-to-high like
greasedlightning) just as we turned the corner of Divinity

avenue i touched the accelerator and give

her the juice, good

                              (it
was the first ride and believe i we was
happy to see how nice she acted right up to
the last minute coming back down by the Public
Gardens i slammed on
the

internalexpanding
&
externalcontracting
brakes Bothatonce and

brought allof her tremB
-ling
to a : dead.

stand-
;Still)

'may i feel said he'

may i feel said he
(i'll squeal said she
just once said he)
it's fun said she

(may i touch said he
how much said she
a lot said he)
why not said she

(let's go said he
not too far said she
what's too far said he
where you are said she)

may i stay said he
(which way said she
like this said he
if you kiss said she

may i move said he
is it love said she)
if you're willing said he
(but you're killing said she

but it's life said he
but your wife said she
now said he)
ow said she

(tiptop said he
don't stop said she
oh no said he)
go slow said she

(cccome? said he
ummm said she)
you're divine! said he
(you are Mine said she)

Robert Graves

born 1895

Down, Wanton, Down!

Down, wanton, down! Have you no shame
That at the whisper of Love's name,
Or Beauty's, presto! up you raise
Your angry head and stand at gaze?

Poor Bombard-captain, sworn to reach
The ravelin and effect a breach –
Indifferent what you storm or why,
So be that in the breach you die!

Love may be blind, but Love at last
Knows what is man and what mere beast;
Or Beauty wayward, but requires
More delicacy from her squires.

Tell me, my witless, whose one boast
Could be your staunchness at the post,
When were you made a man of parts
To think fine and profess the arts?

Will many-gifted Beauty come
Bowing to your bald rule of thumb,
Or Love swear loyalty to your crown?
Be gone, have done! Down, wanton, down!

Anonymous

20th century

This is his life

From 20 to 30 if a man lives right
It is once in the morning and twice at night;
From 30 to 40 if he still lives right
He misses a morning and sometimes a night;

From 40 to 50 it is now and then;
From 50 to 60 it is God knows when;
From 60 to 70 if he is still inclined:
But don't let him kid you, it is still in his mind.
His sporting days are over,
His little light is out;
What used to be his sex appeal
Is now his water spout.
It used to be embarrassing
To make the thing behave
For nearly every morning
It stood and watched him shave.
But now it's getting older,
It sure gives him the blues
To have it dangling down his legs
And watch him clean his shoes.

That Portion of a Woman[41]

That portion of a woman which appeals to man's depravity
Is constructed with extraordinary care,
And what at first appears to be a simple little cavity
Is really an elaborate affair.

Now doctors of distinction have examined these phenomena
On numbers of experimental dames,
And classified the organs of the feminine abdomina
And given them delightful Latin names.

There's the vulva, the vagina, and the jolly old perineum,
And the hymen in the case of many brides;
There are many other gadgets you would love if you could see 'em,
The clitoris and lots of things besides.

So isn't it a pity when we common people chatter
Of the mysteries to which I have referred,
We should use for such a delicate and complicated matter
Such a short and unattractive little word.

O My Darling Flo

O my darling Flo I love you so,
I love you in your nightie;
    When the moonlight flits
    Across your tits
Jesus Christ Almighty!

'Here's to the roses'

Here's to the roses and flowers that bloom,
To me in your arms and you in my room;
A door that is locked and a key that is lost,
And a night that's a thousand years long.

Susanna

Susanna was a lady with plenty of class
Who knocked 'em all dead when she wiggled her
    Eyes at the fellows as girls sometimes do
    To make it quite plain that she's aching to
Take in a movie or go for a sail
And then hurry home for a nice piece of
    Chocolate cake and a slice of roast duck
    For after a meal she was ready to
Go for a ride or a stroll on the dock
With any young man with a sizeable
    Roll of big bills and a pretty good front
    And if he talked fast she would show him her
Little pet dog which was subject to fits
And maybe she'd let him take hold of her
    Lilywhite hands with a movement so quick
    And then she'd reach over and tickle his
Chin while she showed him a trick learned in France
And ask the poor fellow to take off his
    Coat while she sang of the Indian shore
    For whatever she was Susanna was no bore.

A Blue Sea Romance

One very hot day in the summer last year
A young man was seen swimming round Brighton Pier;
He dived underneath it and swam to a rock
And amused all the ladies by shaking his
Fist at a copper who stood on the shore,
The very same copper who copped him before.
    For the policeman to order him out was a farce,
    For the cheeky young man simply showed him his
    Graceful manoeuvres and wonderful pace
    And when once ashore only laughed in his face.

This young man and his sweetheart would go for a swim
And travel some way with his hand on her
Chest to support her should she feel tired,
A kindly attention the lady admired.
    He'd swim like a drake and she like a duck,
    Then finish the morning by having a
    Nice little lunch and a bottle of wine,
    A treat which no lady was known to decline.

Her dress made of serge was the nicest of fits,
And showed to advantage the swell of her
Graceful figure from her head to her feet;
Her appearance, in fact, was exceedingly neat.
    While he lounged on the beach she started to hunt
    For some lovely seaweed to hang round her
    Window at home, a reminder to be
    Of the happy long hours she had spent by the sea.

If for a moment his lady he'd miss
He'd wager his life she was doing a
Kind thoughtful action, by kiss or caress
Soothing some poor little child in distress.
    To return to the story – when eventide falls
    She pleases her boyfriend by tickling his
    Fancy with yarns how the rest of her life
    She'll be to her darling his dear little wife.

He fervently blesses the day he was born,
And all through her kissing he's now got the
Idea in his head that he can't live alone
And as soon as he can he must set up home.

ABC of Love

A is the Artfulness in the words he uses
B is the Blush as she gently refuses
C is the Creep of his hand on her legs
D is the Don't she tearfully begs
E is the Excitement his hand getting higher
F is the Feeling of intense desire
G is the Gasp as her garter he touches
H is how Helpless she feels in his clutches
I is the Itching that makes her feel hot
J is the Jump as he reaches the spot
K is the Kiss with which she rewards him
L is the Love she now feels towards him
M is the Movement they make to the bed
N is the Neat way she opens her legs
O is the Opening that's now revealed
P is the Penis already peeled
Q is the Queer way she feels when it's in
R is the Rapture when sweet pains begin
S is the Stroke getting longer and longer
T is the Throb getting stronger and stronger
U is the Unction that now freely flows
V is the Vim he puts in his blows
W is the Wish for it over again
X is the Xtent of both pleasure and pain
Y is the Yearning that makes her heart throb
Z is the Zambuk he puts on his knob.

'*It is only human nature*'

It is only human nature after all
For a boy to get a girl against a wall
And slip his abomination into her accommodation
To increase the population of the coming generation.

Eskimo Nell

When men grow old and their balls grow cold,
    And the end of their tool turns blue,
Far from that life of Yukon strife
    They'll tell a tale that's true.

So bring me a seat, and buy me a drink,
    And a tale to you I'll tell
Of Deadeye Dick and Mexico Pete
    And a whore named Eskimo Nell.

When Mexico Pete and Deadeye Dick
    Set out in search of fun,
It's Deadeye Dick who wields the prick
    And Mexico Pete the gun.

When Deadeye Dick and the greaser runt
    Were sore distressed and sad
'Twas mostly cunt that bore the brunt
    Though shootings weren't so bad.

When Deadeye Dick and Mexico Pete
    Went down to Deadman's Creek,
They'd had no luck, in the way of a fuck,
    For well nigh over a week,

Bar a moose or two or a caribou
    And a bison cow or so,
But Deadeye Dick was the king of pricks
    And he found such fucking slow.

So Deadeye Dick and Mexico Pete
    Set out for the Rio Grande;
Deadeye Dick with swinging prick,
    And Pete with gun in hand.

And thus they blazed their randy trail,
　　And none their fire withstood,
And many a bride who was hubby's pride
　　Knew pregnant widowhood.

They hit the bank of the Rio Grande
　　At the height of blazing noon
To slake their thirst and do their worst
　　They sought Red Kate's Saloon.

And as they strode into the bar
　　Both prick and gun flashed free:
'According to sex you drunken wrecks,
　　You drinks or fucks with me.'

They knew the fame of our heroes' name
　　From the Horn to Panama
So with little worse than a muttered curse
　　Those dagos lined the bar.

The women knew his playful ways
　　Way down on the Rio Grande
So forty whores tore down their drawers
　　At Deadeye Dick's command.

They saw the fingers of Mexico Pete
　　Touching his pistol grip,
They didn't waste, in frantic haste
　　Those whores began to strip.

Deadeye Dick was breathing hard
　　With noisy snarls and grunts
As forty arses came into view
　　To say nothing of forty cunts.

Now forty arses and forty cunts
　　You'll find, if you use your wits,
And if you're quick at arithmetic,
　　Signifies eighty tits.

Now eighty tits is a goodly sight
　　To a man with a mighty stand;
It may be rare in Berkeley Square
　　But not on the Rio Grande.

Now to test his wind, he'd had a grind
 The previous Saturday night,
And this he'd done to show his fun
 And whet his appetite.

His phallic limb was in fighting trim
 So he backed and took a run,
He took a jump at the nearest rump
 And scored a hole in one.

He bore her to the sandy floor,
 And fairly fucked her fine,
But though she grinned, it put the wind
 Up the other thirtynine.

For when Deadeye Dick performs the trick
 There's scarcely time to spare,
For with speed and strength, on top of length
 He fairly singes hair.

Now Deadeye Dick he fucks 'em quick,
 And has cast the first aside.
He made a dart at the second tart,
 When the swing doors opened wide.

Then entered in that hall of sin,
 Into that house of hell,
A lusty maid, no whit afraid,
 Her name – was Eskimo Nell.

Now Deadeye Dick had got his prick
 Well into number two
When Eskimo Nell let out a yell
 And called to him 'Hi You!'

He gave a flick of his muscular prick
 And the whore flew over his head,
He turned about with a snarl and a shout
 And his face and his knob were red.

Eskimo Nell she stood it well
 As she looked between his eyes.
She glanced with scorn upon his horn
 Steaming between his thighs.

She stubbed out the butt of her cigarette
   On the end of his gleaming knob,
And so utterly beat was Mexico Pete
   That he quite forgot his job.

It was Eskimo Nell who was first to speak,
   In accents clear and cool,
'You cuntstruck shrimp of a Yankee pimp
   Do you call that thing a tool?

And if this here town can't take it down,'
   She sneered at the cowering whores,
'Here's a cunt that can do the stunt:
   Eskimo Nell, for yours!'

She removed her garments one by one
   With an air of conscious pride
Till there she stood in her womanhood
   And they saw the Great Divide.

'Tis fair to state 'twas not so great
   Though its strength lay well within
And a better word, that's often heard,
   Would not be *cunt* but *quim*.

She laid her down on the tabletop
   Whereon was set a glass,
With a flick of her tits she ground it to bits
   Between the cheeks of her arse.

She bent her knees with supple ease
   And spread them wide apart,
And with smiling nods to the randy sods
   She gave him the cue to start.

But Deadeye Dick, he knew a trick
   Or two, and he took his time,
For a miss like this was perfect bliss
   So he played in a pantomime.

He flicked his foreskin up and down
   He made his balls inflate
Until they resembled two granite knobs
   Upon a garden gate.

He winked his arsehole in and out
    And his balls increased in size;
His mighty prick grew twice as thick
    And nearly reached his eyes.

He polished it well with alcohol,
    To get it steaming hot,
And to finish the job, he peppered the knob
    With the cayenne pepper pot.

He didn't back and take a run,
    Or make a flying leap,
He didn't swoop, but made a stoop,
    And a steady forward creep.

With peering eyes he took a sight
    Along that fearsome tool,
And the long slow glide as it slid inside
    Was calculating – cool.

Now you all have seen the pistons gleam
    On the mighty CPR
With the driving force of a thousand horse
    So you know what pistons are.

Or you think you do, if you've yet to view
    The power that drives the prick,
Or the work that's done on a nonstop run,
    By a man like Deadeye Dick.

None but a fool would challenge his tool,
    No thinking man would doubt
For his fame increased as the Great High Priest
    Of the ceaseless in-and-out.

But Eskimo Nell was an infidel
    And equalled a whole harem,
With the strength of ten in her abdomen,
    And a Rock of Ages' beam.

Amidships she could stand a rush
    Like the flush of a water closet,
So she gripped his cock like the Chatwood lock
    Of the National Safe Deposit.

But Deadeye Dick would not come quick,
    He meant to conserve his powers,
When in the mind he'd grind and grind
    For more than a couple of hours.

She lay a while with a subtle smile
    And then her grip grew keener,
And with a sigh she sucked him dry
    With the ease of a vacuum cleaner.

She did this feat in a way so neat
    As to set at grand defiance
The primary cause of the basic laws
    That govern all sexual science.

She simply rode that phallic tool,
    That for years had stood the test,
And accepted rules of the ancient schools
    In a second or two went west!

And now my friend we near the end
    Of this copulative epic
For the effect on Dick was so sudden and quick
    'Twas akin to an anaesthetic.

He slid to the floor, and knew no more,
    His passion extinct and dead.
He didn't shout as his tool slipped out
    'Though 'tis said she'd stripped the thread.

Then Mexico Pete, he rose to his feet
    To avenge his friend's affront
And his tough-nosed colt with a savage jolt
    He rammed right up her cunt.

He shoved it hard to the trigger guard
    And fired it twice times three
But to his surprise she closed her eyes
    And squealed in ecstasy.

As she rose to her feet, she looked so sweet
    'Bully!' she cried, 'for you;
Though I might have guessed it's about the best
    That you poor sods could do.'

When next, my friends, you two intend
    To sally forth for fun,
Get Deadeye Dick a sugar stick
    And buy yourself a bun.

For I'm away to the frozen North,
    Where pricks are big and strong,
Back to the land of the frozen stand
    Where the nights are six months long.

When you stick it in it's as hard as sin,
    In a land where spunk is spunk,
Not a trickling stream of lukewarm cream
    But a solid frozen chunk.

Back to the land where they understand
    What it means to copulate,
Where even the dead lie two in a bed
    And the children masturbate.

Back once more to the sins of men,
    To the Land of the Midnight Sun,
I go to spend a worthy end
    For the north is calling '*Come !*'

Pablo Neruda
1904–73

Lone Gentleman

Young homosexuals and girls in love,
and widows gone to seed, sleepless, delirious,
and novice housewives pregnant some thirty hours,
the hoarse cats cruising across my garden's shadows
like a necklace of throbbing, sexual oysters
surround my solitary home
like enemies entrenched against my soul,
like conspirators in pyjamas
exchanging long, thick kisses on the sly.

The radiant summer entices lovers here
in melancholic regiments
made up of fat and flabby, gay and mournful couples:
under the graceful palm trees, along the moonlit beach,
there is a continual excitement of trousers and petticoats,
the crisp sound of stockings caressed,
women's breasts shining like eyes.

It's quite clear that the local clerk, bored to the hilt,
after his weekday tedium, cheap paperbacks in bed,
has managed to make his neighbour
and he takes her to the miserable flea-pits
where the heroes are young stallions or passionate princes:
he caresses her legs downy with soft hair
with his wet, hot hands smelling of cigarillos.

Seducer's afternoons and strictly legal nights
fold together like a pair of sheets, burying me:
the siesta hours when young male and female students
as well as priests retire to masturbate,
and when animals screw outright,
and bees smell of blood and furious flies buzz,
and cousins play kinkily with their girl cousins,
and doctors glare angrily at their young patient's husband,
and the professor, almost unconsciously, during the morning hours,
copes with his marital duties and then has breakfast,
and, later on, the adulterers who love each other with real love,
on beds as high and spacious as sea-going ships –
so for sure and for ever this great forest surrounds me,
breathing through flowers large as mouths chock full of teeth,
black-rooted in the shapes of hoofs and shoes.

Vladimir Holan

born 1905

The Virgin

The party is over at which there were so many lights
the dark was perfect.
And he was there. She didn't mind
if his feelings were wine and his thoughts
grapes.
Towards morning he left her. She sat gazing
through the small hole in her dress
at Monday's naked nail.

George Barker

born 1913

from *The True Confession of George Barker*

The act of human procreation
   – The rutting tongue, the grunt and shudder,
The sweat, the reek of defecation,
   The cradle hanging by the bladder,
The scramble up the hairy ladder,
   And from the thumping bed of Time
Immortality, a white slime,
   Sucking at its mother's udder –

The act of human procreation
   – The sore dug plugging, the lugged-out bub,
The small man priming a lactation,
   The grunt, the drooping teat, the rub
Of gum and dug, the slobbing kiss:
   Behold the mater amabilis,
Sow with a saviour, messiah and cow,
   Virgin and piglet, son and sow:

The act of human procreation,
   – O crown and flower, O culmination
Of perfect love throughout creation –
   What can I compare to it?
O eternal butterflies in the belly,
O trembling of the heavenly jelly,
O miracle of birth! Really
   We are excreted, like shit.

Dylan Thomas
1914–53

Light breaks where no sun shines

Light breaks where no sun shines;
Where no sea runs, the waters of the heart
Push in their tides;
And, broken ghosts with glow-worms in their heads,
The things of light
File through the flesh where no flesh decks the bones.

A candle in the thighs
Warms youth and seed and burns the seeds of age;
Where no seed stirs,
The fruit of man unwrinkles in the stars,
Bright as a fig;
Where no wax is, the candle shows its hairs.

Dawn breaks behind the eyes;
From poles of skull and toe the windy blood
Slides like a sea;
Nor fenced, nor staked, the gushers of the sky
Spout to the rod
Divining in a smile the oil of tears.

Night in the sockets rounds,
Like some pitch moon, the limit of the globes;
Day lights the bone;

Where no cold is, the skinning gales unpin
The winter's robes;
The film of spring is hanging from the lids.

Light breaks on secret lots,
On tips of thought where thoughts smell in the rain;
When logics die,
The secret of the soil grows through the eye,
And blood jumps in the sun;
Above the waste allotments the dawn halts.

Gavin Ewart
born 1916

Miss Twye

Miss Twye was soaping her breasts in her bath
When she heard behind her a meaning laugh
And to her amazement she discovered
A wicked man in the bathroom cupboard.

Short Story

She bit his love-nuts, what a nasty girl!

Her two were always going before her
a perfect pair, so softly supported.

They met in a bar and he was explaining
how 'Baa, Baa, Black Sheep!' is about pubic hair
and how the clitoris is only really
the little boy who lives down the lane.

Stand in front of the mirror and let me lick you.

It was hot on the beach. Too many bikinis
and several hangovers were stretched out in the sun.

They drank a very cold white wine. It
was a great life. After a big lunch
they rolled about on a 42 square foot bed.
Some sand grated into their copulations.

There's a whole literature of the Mediterranean.

He and She and a sea that is tideless
and peaches that ought to be wearing frilly panties.

He was called Jan and she was called Paula.
The Loves were laughing when they got together,
they parted with a shrill cry and a strong backhand
that reddened with a line her bloated floaters.

James Kirkup
born 1923

Love in a Space Suit

Dear, when on some distant planet
We, love's protestants, alight,
How, in our deep-space-diver suits
Shall our devoted limbs unite?

You shall have those ruby lips
In a helmet-bowl, inverted
On your golden locks, enclosed:
Your starry eyes shall be inserted
In a plastic contact-vizor
To keep out the stellar cold.
And your teeth of pearls shall chatter
On a tongue too hot to hold.

Dear, those pretty little fingers
Shall be cased with lead around,
And your snowy breasts, my dove,
With insulating tape be bound.

There your lovely legs, my sweet
In asbestos boots shall stump;
And a grim all-metal corset
Shall depress that witty rump.

How shall I, in suits of iron
Or of aluminium
Communicate my body's fire
In love's planetarium?
Darling, must we kiss by knocking
Bowl on bowl, a glassy bliss?
Must we lie apart for aye,
Not far, but not as near as this?

Nay! before I will renounce
My lust for earth and love of you,
I shall have us both, dear, fitted
With a space suit made for two.

Robin Skelton
born 1925

Her leather coat

Her leather coat
shone in the sun. She threw
one booted leg across
the other, lit
a cigarette, leaned back.
The leather creaked.
She said, 'I bet
you'd have a bloody fit

if I said that I'm very
good in bed
and really fancy
doing it with you!'

I sat upon the terrace edge.
I said,
'I'm really not quite certain
what I'd do –

but I am sure I wouldn't
have a fit.'
Below the parapet
the cliff dropped sheer
in hacked confusion to the sea.
I said,
'I might leap at the chance
or, perhaps, off here!'

and smiled at her.
She shuddered and smiled back.
'It's bright outside,' she said,
'but still too cold
to sit out long. Can we
go in the house?'
I said, 'The Spring
is only three days old –

we mustn't be impatient!'
At the door
she turned and laid
one black precarious glove
against my cheek. She muttered,
'Spring is Hell
if you are good in bed
but bad at love!'

You were ashamed

You were ashamed
of the soft down on your bottom,
I of my member's
huge-bulbed gracelessness:
delicately I caressed
that delicate bottom;

graciously you rewarded
gracelessness.

Never were two more suited,
each one's shame
answered with, first, affection,
then desire:
now I lie sleepless
dwelling on your shame,
and shamelessly desiring
your desire.

Christopher Logue
born 1926

from *New Numbers*

Moonlight. Midnight.
A tall girl sways on the brow of an empty motorway.

Four huge sausages rise behind.
The light is like a red-hot body rub.

'Dance naked for me, girl,' the eldest cries.
'Or I will make a reasonable compromise.'

The girl takes off her dress.
Headlights reveal her glamour.
Her coral reeks of musk.

'Let me imagine,' says the next, 'I lead
loose, tantalizing pinks
across your meadows.'

The girl turns round.
She rubs her body with her hands.

'SUCK THIS! SUCK THIS!'
The third huge sausage cries.
Police cars draw their blue patrol lamps by.

The fourth is young and blind.

'Girl, follow me.
Laughing I roll into obscurity.'

They leave.

Thom Gunn
born 1929

The Discovery of the Pacific

They lean against the cooling car, backs pressed
Upon the dusts of a brown continent,
And watch the sun, now Westward of their West,
Fall to the ocean. Where it led they went.

Kansas to California. Day by day
They travelled emptier of the things they knew.
They improvised new habits on the way,
But lost the occasions, and then lost them too.

One night, no-one and nowhere, she had woken
To resin-smell and to the firs' slight sound,
And through their sleeping-bag had felt the broken
Tight-knotted surfaces of the naked ground.

Only his quiet body cupping hers
Kept her from it, the extreme chill. By degrees
She fell asleep. Around them in the firs
The wind probed, tiding through forked estuaries.

And now their skin is caked with road, the grime
Merely reflecting sunlight as it fails.
They leave their clothes among the rocks they climb,
Blunt leaves of iceplant nuzzle at their soles.

Now they stand chin-deep in the sway of ocean,
Firm West, two stringy bodies face to face,
And come, together, in the water's motion,
The full caught pause of their embrace.

Ted Hughes
born 1930

A Childish Prank

Man's and woman's bodies lay without souls,
Dully gaping, foolishly staring, inert
On the flowers of Eden.
God pondered.

The problem was so great, it dragged him asleep.

Crow laughed.
He bit the Worm, God's only son,
Into two writhing halves.

He stuffed into man the tail half
With the wounded end hanging out.

He stuffed the head half headfirst into woman
And it crept in deeper and up
To peer out through her eyes
Calling its tail-half to join up quickly, quickly
Because O it was painful.

Man awoke being dragged across the grass.
Woman awoke to see him coming.
Neither knew what had happened.

God went on sleeping.

Crow went on laughing.

Adrian Mitchell
born 1932

Celia Celia

When I am sad and weary,
When I think all hope has gone,
When I walk along High Holborn
I think of you with nothing on.

Tom Stothert
born 1933

Chagrin

Odd it is so easy
    when it is hard
        and tonight it was so hard
           when it was soft.

Old proverb updated

Yes, love did get under my skin. But then Venus
    is pretty . . .
            . . . intravenous.

heartbroken

sadly though I was all Is for you
  you had no yous for me at all

Highway girl

You had only,
            to see her,
                        look at you,
                                    to feel a shiver,
as she made you,
            want to,
                        stand (there),
                                    and deliver.

Every hymn's for some her

We have this   sort
            of Hindu   relationship
I have
            my Tantra   and she has
her tantrums   and
            somehow   sex
between us   both is all
            rite.

Michael Horovitz
born 1935

*EpithaLAY-ME-**ON**–um–um . . .*
(*An Immodest Proposition : may be sung – to
tune of 'Habañera' in* Carmen)

  Snip my parsley
Bake my bean
Wash my pants –
Be my queen

– Sniff my snout
& Stick my wicket
– I'll expand ye grout
& Fill thy bucket

– Nip your cherry
Bite your bud,
Churn your milk
To cheesy mud
– Spill your beans
& Spring your trap,
Swill your juice
& Sluice your pap!

Vamp & munch
– Stomp 'n' crunch,
Do yer thing
– Rock & swing

   – Let's
Strip the bench,
Hump the lunch

– Pump the park
& Swallow the dark
– Heat the grove
& Eat the stove,
Ready the nerve

– O taste the love!

Sip at the doormat
Guzzle the door
– Gobble the neighbours
& Goose the law

– Season the swamp,
Gorged on desire . . . .

Lap up the bedstead,
Chew the clock
Wallow thy wombhead
Kiss my cock –

   Unbind this mind
Peel my rind
Cook my goose
& Let me loose –

When your lover
Has gone away
You'll find you're left
With the frying pan –

When you've fallen
Into the fire
You find you can't
Get up any higher –

Roger McGough
born 1937

At Lunchtime – A Story of Love

When the busstopped suddenly to avoid
damaging a mother and child in the road, the
younglady in the greenhat sitting opposite
was thrown across me, and not being one to
miss an opportunity i started to makelove
with all my body.

At first she resisted saying that it
was tooearly in the morning and toosoon
after breakfast and that anyway she found
me repulsive. But when I explained that
this being a nuclearage, the world was going
to end at lunchtime, she tookoff her
greenhat, put her busticket in her pocket
and joined in the exercise.

The buspeople, and therewere many of
them, were shockedandsurprised and amused-
andannoyed, but when the word got around
that the world was coming to an end at lunch-
time, they put their pride in their pockets
with their bustickets and madelove one with
the other. And even the busconductor, being

over, climbed into the cab and struck up
some sort of relationship with the driver.

Thatnight, on the bus coming home,
wewere all alittle embarrassed, especially me
and the young lady in the greenhat, and we
all started to say in different ways howhasty
and foolish we had been. Butthen, always
having been a bitofalad, i stood up and
said it was a pity that the world didn't nearly
end every lunchtime and that we could always
pretend. And then it happened . . .

Quick asa crash we all changed partners
and soon the bus was aquiver with white
mothballbodies doing naughty things.

> And the next day
> And everyday
> In everybus
> In everystreet
> In everytown
> In everycountry

people pretended that the world was coming
to an end at lunchtime. It still hasn't.
Although in a way it has.

Teresinka Pereira
born 1940

Narcissus Woman
I have masturbated so much that by now I am madly in love with
myself. I am a young woman, beautiful, I have longings and desires,
I live life intensely. I take pleasure in myself. In my life, I have been
married, muffled, lesbianized, communized. A year ago I got my
first taste of independence. One day I came home after spending ten
days at a commune. It was my final attempt to establish a love bond

with somebody else. Eight of us lived out those ten days together, four men and four women, women, we paired off with this person, that person, women or men. At the end of ten days, I was frazzled, exhausted, grown weary of everyone, still unfulfilled and worse: bored! There was nothing left for me to try in sex, I would shut myself up in my house and vow never again to go out.

First I meandered my way through the garden, looking at flowers, searching for some new thing bowed down beneath all the honeysuckle bloom. Enveloped in flowery fragrance, I felt myself thinking, this must be how virgins breathe, there was no other way to explain that magic that anoints them at birth. As for myself, I have the uneasy suspicion that I never was a virgin. One day, in my sleep, I listened to my mother reproaching my father with raping me while I was still in her womb. I only remember that when I was born I had a spikenard between my legs, instead of a vulva like other girls. My parents, dying of shame, decided to shuttle me off to Europe for some never-too-clear operation, which left the first terrible mark on my childhood.

Thinking back to those times threw me into such strange contradictions, I decided to turn from the honeysuckle and walk to the door of my house, resolved to go inside, saying my blissful, last, definite, mortal goodbye to the outside world.

My mother was right. I should have gone through life with a spikenard for a vulva and never again would I have all these many troubles. Spikenards have such a simple approach to love.

Wendy Perriam
born 1940

A silent movie

How dare you make love to me like that,
in that cold, silent, uncommitted way,
using your prick like a mechanical pumping-engine
and thinking of *Playboy*.

I'm hot and wet, man,
opening like a Venus Flytrap,
streaming from all orifices
and screaming with agonizing
life-enhancing, mad, entrancing
cunt-enchanting
joy.
And there you lie,
worrying about the next-door-neighbours
and wishing the bed springs wouldn't creak
and refusing to bloody well SPEAK.
And when I bite your thighs
you're praying that the marks won't show
when you have to strip for your daily dip
in the city gym –
(must keep fit) –
You hypocrite!

Quick!
I want your rough beard
to lacerate my breasts,
but you turn away
and say you prefer it the back way,
that's fatal
because it's so damned good
I'm shouting more and hotting up the pace,
but at least that way
I cannot see the fury on your face.
You Woman hater!

Oh, I'm really away now
(bugger the neighbours!)
Your piston-engine prick
is tearing the living daylights out of me
and I'm wild with it,
but why don't you bloody well
SAY SOMETHING?
Are you enjoying it, damn you,
or are you just a machine

that's wound up
and forgotten the words?
I remember past loves,
past beds,
and the torrent of fire and honey
from the mouths of wild
and wonderful men
who knew how to love
with lungs
as well as loins,
and the sticky plethora
of kisses over and under
drowning sounds
so lewd and beautiful
that all my heart and cunt
were burning equally.

Oh you cold, stingy
uptight, unyielding sod,
how do I know
whether my ecstasy
is boring the pants off you
(forgive the pun),
or whether your fastidious
distaste is aimed at me
specifically,
or at the whole race of
swallowing, wallowing women
and wanton cunts,
or whether you yearn
for an ice maiden
or a marble goddess,
or for that dreadful Mrs Lloyd
who wears hats
and doesn't like it.

All right, you've come now
(silently)
and you've shuffled off
looking slightly out-of-sorts

and embarrassed by that
ill-bred piston-engine which *will*
take you unawares
despite your finer feelings.
And of course you wouldn't kiss me
or say it was wonderful,
but hurried off to wash,
remembering germs
that lurk in private places
and nasty notices
in public lavatories.

I'm clean, damn you,
but I won't be for long
if you go on insulting me
with your cold and disapproving
silence.
I'm still going, still
coming, still pounding out
gorgeous obscenities
in our sweaty, unhygienic
incorrigibly creaking
bed.
And there you are
washing my cunt away
with Wright's Coal Tar
(drop dead!)
and gargling away
the taste of me
with Dettol.

Look here, old sport,
I warn you,
when I'm through here
I'm going to sleep with every
man, boy and tramp
I can lay my filthy paws on.
Painters, plumbers,
unshaven bummers,
mad Irish labourers

and men who read meters,
I'm going to drain their last-gasp drop
(DON'T STOP!)
and make my life's work
having it away,
and let's hope, by God,
they know their way about a woman
and what's a damned sight more important,
they don't forget
the words that fit the play.

Erica Jong •

born 1942

The Long Tunnel of Wanting You

This is the long tunnel of wanting you.
Its walls are lined with remembered kisses
wet & red as the inside of your mouth,
full & juicy as your probing tongue,
warm as your belly against mine,
deep as your navel leading home,
soft as your sleeping cock beginning to stir,
tight as your legs wrapped around mine,
straight as your toes pointing toward the bed
as you roll over & thrust your hardness
into the long tunnel of my wanting,
seeding it with dreams & unbearable hope,
making memories of the future,
straightening out my crooked past,
teaching me to live in the present present tense
with the past perfect and the uncertain future
suddenly certain for certain
in the long tunnel of my old wanting
which before always had an ending
but now begins & begins again
with you, with you, with you.

The Wingless & The Winged

the wingless thing
man . . .

– e. e. cummings

Most men use their cocks
for two things only:
they stand up pissing
& lie down fucking.
The world is full of horizontal men –
or vertical ones –
& really it is all the same disease.

But your cock flies
over the earth,
making shadows
on the bodies of women,
making wild bird noises
from its tiny mouth,
making music
& food for thought.
It is not a wingless thing
at all.

We could call it Pegasus –
if it didn't make us think
of gas stations.
Or we could call it Icarus –
if it didn't make us think
of falling.

But still it dips & dives
through the sky like a glider,
in search of a meadow,
a field,
a sun-dappled swamp
from which (you rightly said)
all life begins.

Alan Bold

born 1943

The Coming of the Vision

This certain year
Everything became a blur
For a long, wayward, witching spell:
Things were going well
One second, and the next
I was down, distant, poleaxed.
Why?
That was the question I
Asked myself; why now, this moment,
When I was free from sentiment?
The answer was love –
I was not getting enough.
You know what I mean?
Up beyond the barleyfield the lean
Roe-deer were wild with passion
And, in their delicate fashion,
Making love with each other,
Bending with the weather.
That was the reason:
Love was in season.
Things I needed
To see simply receded
Into a vision of all all-embracing female
With a lascivious smile
And a body so sensuously curved
It might have been carved
From the original idea of womanhood,
A notion of a tall tempting nude
With every orifice
In the right place
And the ultimate entrance
Like something in a trance
Waiting to enmesh
Me in pulsating flesh.

This vision rose into the skies
Provoking trembling sighs
And near-seizures; the thighs,
When they moved, caressed
Each other while the rest
Of the perfection merged with all:
There was the small
Indentation behind the knee,
The shimmering skintight ecstasy
Of the belly which
Went down, down, down into a rich
Clutch of curly hair
Which seemed to disappear
Into the glistening world beyond;
And
This deliciously wet
Target
Was surrounded by more curves
And more curves and more curves
Until
The incredible thrill
Of the vision made it real,
Something to feel
With every particle,
Something of a miracle,
But here, real, now,
No titillating sacred cow
Beyond the ken
Of men
But a real woman
For a real man.
The breasts were supple
And each stiffened nipple
Could be fingered and thumbed
While the waist succumbed
To a rubbing motion
That transferred emotion
To the whole world below

Where a slow
Rhythm began
And again and again
Got faster,
Got moister,
Until you could taste her
Inner fire,
The end of desire,
The beginning of love,
The birthplace of life,
The perfect situation
For prolonged penetration.
The vision lay down in the grass,
An embodiment of Yes,
And
I took my stand
To push
Past the bush
And feel whole
In this small
World that could swell
To a universal
Implosion, a sweet
Fusion of energy and heat.
I had forgotten that blur,
I had left it in her
And found my self.

Acknowledgements

For permission to include items in this anthology acknowledgement is made as follows:

A. J. Arberry for a translation of Imr Al-Qais from *The Seven Odes* to George Allen and Unwin Ltd;

George Barker for an extract from *The True Confession of George Barker* to MacGibbon & Kee Ltd/Granada Publishing Ltd;

Oliver Bernard for a translation of Apollinaire from *Selected Poems* (Penguin Modern Poets, 1965) to Penguin Books Ltd, © Oliver Bernard 1965;

Alan Bold for a poem to the author;

Karen Brazell for a translation from *The Confessions of Lady Nijo* to Peter Owen Ltd;

John Brough for three translations from *Poems from the Sanskrit* (Penguin Classics, 1968) to Penguin Books Ltd, © John Brough 1968;

e. e. cummings for two poems from *Collected Poems* to MacGibbon & Kee Ltd/Granada Publishing Ltd;

Rubén Dario for a poem from *Selected Poems* to the translator Lysander Kemp and the University of Texas Press;

Margaret Diesendorf for a translation of Gottfried Benn to the translator and to Verlag Max Niedermayer, Munich;

Alistair Elliot for four Aretino translations and one Marino translation to the translator, for six Verlaine translations to the translator and Anvil Press;

Gavin Ewart for two poems to the author;

Robert Graves for a poem from *Collected Poems* to Cassell and Co Ltd;

Peter Green for a translation of Archilochus to the translator, to David Higham Associates and to the *Times Literary Supplement*;

Thom Gunn for a poem from *Moly* to Faber and Faber Ltd;

Dr P. J. W. Higson for three D'Annunzio translations to the translator;

Vladimir Holan for a poem from *Selected Poems* (Penguin Modern European Poets, 1971) to the author, the translators (Jarmila and Ian Milner) and to Penguin Books Ltd, © Vladimir Holan 1971, translation © Jarmila and Ian Milner 1971;

Michael Horovitz for a poem from *Love Poems* (*New Departures* No. 9) to the author;

Ted Hughes for a poem from *Crow* to Faber and Faber Ltd;

Erica Jong for two poems from *Selected Poems* to the author and A. D. Peters & Co Ltd;

James Kirkup for a poem from *Descent Into The Cave* to the author;

Christopher Logue for an extract from *New Numbers* to Hope Leresche and Sayle, © Christopher Logue 1969;

Hugh MacDiarmid for two poems to the author's Estate;

Roger McGough for a poem from *Penguin Modern Poets 10* to the author and Hope Leresche and Sayle, © Roger McGough 1967;

James Michie for three translations from *The Poems of Catullus* to Rupert Hart-Davis Ltd/Granada Publishing Ltd;

Adrian Mitchell for a poem from *Out Loud* to Cape Goliard Press;

Pablo Neruda for a poem from *Selected Poems* to the translator (Nathaniel Tarn), Jonathan Cape Ltd and the Estate of Pablo Neruda;

Teresinka Pereira for a poem, to the author and translator (Naomi Lindstrom);

Wendy Perriam for a poem, to the author;

Robert Reeves for a translation of Martial to the translator;

Ralph Russell and Khurshidul Islam for a translation from *Three Mughal Poets* to the translators and George Allen and Unwin Ltd;

Beram Saklatvala for a translation from Villon's *Poems* (Everyman's Library) to the translator and J. M. Dent and Sons Ltd;

Hugh J. Schonfield for an extract from *The Song of Songs* to the translator and Mark Paterson and Associates;

Robin Skelton for two poems from *Because of Love* to the author and McClelland and Stewart Ltd; for seven translations from *Two Hundred Poems from the Greek Anthology* to the author and A. P. Watt Ltd;

Tom Stothert for five poems to the author;

Dylan Thomas for a poem from *Collected Poems* to J. M. Dent and Sons Ltd and the Trustees for the Copyrights of the Late Dylan Thomas;

Louis Untermeyer for a translation from *The Poetry and Prose of Heinrich Heine* to the editor (Frederic Ewan) and The Citadel Press;

W. B. Yeats for a poem from *Collected Poems* to M. B. Yeats, Miss Anne Yeats and the Macmillan Co of London and Basingstoke.

Notes on the Text

As my editorial intention is to bring erotic verse within the reach of the general public my priority has been to make the poems easily accessible. To this end I have modernized spelling, though, in the case of a poet like Herrick who minutely supervised his work through the press, I have respected individual punctuation as meaningful. Rather than thematically comparmentalizing the text I have settled for a chronological presentation so the poems can speak for themselves in the context of their own period. Where extracts are used, asterisks denote omissions. I have not thought it necessary to give a precise bibliographical reference for each entry: the established poets are easily approachable in collected editions, lesser-known poets are found in anthologies relating to the relevant century (e.g. the *Oxford* books of verse), and the modern poets are covered by the list of Acknowledgements. Many of the older anonymous poems survive in manuscripts, ephemeral publications and broadsheets. A detailed list of seventeenth-century sources is included in John Wardroper's anthology *Love and Drollery* (London, 1969) while valuable popular and broadside literature is collected in V. de Sola Pinto and A. E. Rodway's *The Common Muse* (London, 1957). The anonymous nineteenth-century work is of two types. First, seven poems ('The Origin of Species' to 'Facetiae') are urban bawdry taken from the monthly Victorian journal *The Pearl* which ran from July 1879 to December 1880 – an omnibus edition was published in London in 1975. Then there are rural pieces which have been orally transmitted since the nineteenth century. One of these ('The Pitman's Lovesong') is given in A. L. Lloyd's *Folk Song in England* (London, 1967) and the six remaining nineteenth-century anonymous texts are performed by twentieth-century singers on *The Folk Songs of Britain, Volume 2*, 1961 (Topic Records 12T158). The anonymous twentieth-century work was collected after I appealed in several places (*New Statesman, Tribune, TLS, Observer, The Scotsman*) for such material and I would like to thank Alex Bridge, J. P. Bridger, Henry Cowper, Frank Holland and S. W. Nelki for communicating texts to me. The following notes are purely informative and I have placed them here rather than burdening the text with footnotes.

Archilochus

1 p. 33 *Epode*: NEOBULE, with whom Archilochus had a disastrous affair, was the daughter of Lycambes.

Theocritus

2 p. 37 *Daphnis*: LUCINA is goddess of light.

Catullus

3 p. 41 *'Cato, it's ludicrous'*: CATO is Valerius Cato, a fellow poet.
4 p. 42 *'The Lesbia'*: LESBIA was the great love of Catullus's life, though, as is obvious from the poem, the affair turned sour; Lesbia has been identified as Clodia, the wife of Q. Metellus Celer who became governor of North Italy in 63BC.

Ovid

5 p. 43 *'Your husband will be with us'*: HIPPODAMIA was the wife of Pirithous at whose nuptials the battle between the Centaurs and Lapithae was fought.
6 p. 46 *'In summer's heat'*: SEMIRAMIS was the legendary empress of Nineveh (associated with the hanging gardens of Babylon).
7-10 p. 49 *'Either she was foul'*: PYLIUS refers to Nestor (king of Pylos) who lived to a great age; TITHON is Tithonus to whom the gods granted immortality but not eternal youth; PHEMIUS is a musician in the Odyssey; THAMYRIS is a blind Thracian musician in the Iliad.

Martial

11 p. 56 *'Wife there are some points'*: HECTOR, the great Trojan hero, was the wife of ANDROMACHE; PENELOPE became a symbol of marital fidelity by rejecting the advances of various suitors during the twenty-year homecoming of her husband ULYSSES, king of Ithaca; JULIA, daughter of CAESAR, married POMPEY in 59 BC and died in childbirth in 54 BC; PORTIA was the wife of BRUTUS, one of Caesar's assassins; JUPITER, Roman god of heaven and consort of JUNO, queen of heaven, took the beautiful mortal GANYMEDE as his cupbearer; according to tradition the rape of LUCRECE, the Roman matron, by Sextus Tarquinius led to the establishment of the Roman republic in 509 BC; LAIS was a celebrated Greek courtesan.

Juvenal

12-14 pp. 58-60 *'If then thy lawful spouse'*: TILLER is a cabinet drawer; ERINGOES are roots of the sea holly thought to have aphrodisiac powers; NESTOR, king of Pylos, was supposed to have lived to a great age.

Bhartrhari and Amaru

15 p. 62 Given the nature of Sanskrit anthologies it is notoriously difficult to attribute individual poems to individual authors; Bhartrhari and Amaru, however, demonstrate distinct poetic personalities.

Donne

16–18 pp. 95–6 *Love's Progress*: REMORA is a sucking fish formerly believed to stop ships by attaching its sucker; SESTOS AND ABYDOS were two towns facing each other across the narrowest part of the Hellespont; CLYSTER is a liquid injected into the intestines.

Rochester

For the following notes on Rochester, I am indebted to David M. Vieth's edition of *The Complete Poems of John Wilmot, Earl of Rochester* (New Haven and London, 1968).

19–21 p. 127 *The Imperfect Enjoyment*: STEW is a brothel; WEEPINGS refers to moisture discharged from the body; STRANGURY is agonizing urination; STONE is gallstone.

22–32 pp. 128–31 *A Ramble in St James's Park*: THE BEAR was an ordinary in Drury Lane; ARETINE is Pietro Aretino; BULK is a bench in front of a shop; CARMEN are carriers; KNIGHTS O' TH'ELBOW are gamblers; SLUR is a method of cheating at dice; MOTHER OF THE MAIDS was Lady Bridget Sanderson (1592–1682), mother of the maids of honour to Queen Catherine from 1669; SIR EDWARD SUTTON (d. 1695) was Gentleman of the Privy Chamber in Ordinary to the King; BANSTEAD in Surrey was associated with the raising of sheep and was near Epsom racecourse much frequented by Charles II; JOB is a thrust; PLAYED BOOTY means they ganged up on each other; SURFEIT WATER was a medicinal drink thought to cure hangovers.

33 p. 132 *Signior Dildo*: this was written after the arrival in London on 26 November 1673 of Mary of Modena for her personal – subsequent to the Italian proxy – marriage to James, Duke of York; ST JAMES'S STREET was the home of the Duke and Duchess of York; LADY SOUTHESK, daughter of the Duke of Hamilton and wife of Robert, 3rd Earl of Southesk, was famed for her promiscuity; LADY SUFFOLK – Barbara, wife of the 3rd Earl of Suffolk, was Groom of the Stole to Queen Catherine; LADY BETTY was Lady Elizabeth Howard, daughter of Lady Suffolk; COUNTESS OF FALMOUTH was Mary, widow of Charles Berkeley (1st Earl of Falmouth) who was killed in the sea battle against the Dutch on 3 June 1665; COUNTESS OF RALPH was Elizabeth, widow of Joceline Percy (Earl of Northumberland, d. 1670); on 24 August 1673 she married Ralph Montague, later Earl and Duke of Montague; THE FIERCE HARRYS refers to Rochester's friend Henry Saville who in September 1671 had to flee after being found in the countess of Northumberland's bedchamber; HER GRACE OF CLEVELAND was Barbara Palmer, Duchess of Cleveland and nymphomaniac mistress of Charles II; DUCHESS OF MODENA was Duchess Laura, Regent of Modena, mother of the new Duchess of York; COUNTESS O'TH'COCKPIT was Nell Gwyn, the Cockpit being part of Whitehall Palace; RED HOWARD, RED SHELDON, AND TEMPLE SO TALL: Ann Howard, Frances Sheldon, Philippa Temple were Maids of Honour to the Queen; SIGNIOR BERNARD was Don Bernardo de Salinas, Spanish diplomat; DOLL HOWARD was Dorothy, elder sister of Ann Howard, and also a Maid of Honour to the Queen; ST ALBANS was Henry Jermyn, Earl of St Albans (d. 1684), Lord Chamberlain; BORGO, a town near Modena; THE FOREMAN OF SHOPS were the puritan merchants of London usually caricatured as cuckolds; BURNING THE POPE AND HIS NEPHEW DILDO – papal effigies were frequently burned by anti-Catholic Londoners and a letter to Rochester from Henry Savile (26 January 1670) tells of customs officers burning a box of imported dildoes; TOM KILLIGREW'S WIFE: Thomas Killigrew, dramatist and manager of the King's House, married Charlotte, daughter of John de Hesse, and she became Keeper of the Sweet Coffer for the Queen in 1662 and First Lady of the Queen's Privy Chamber on 4 June 1662; MADAM KNIGHT was a musical mistress of Charles II; CAZZO is colloquial Italian for penis; LADY SANDYS was a friend of Nell Gwyn.

34 p. 136 *On Cary Frazier*: Cary was a Maid of Honour to Queen Catherine and a beautiful ornamental presence in Charles II's court; her father was Sir Alexander Frazier, the King's Principal Physician and her mother was one of the Queen's Dressers.

Anonymous

35 p. 145 '*She lay all naked*': THE CYPRIAN DAME is Venus, THE BOY is Adonis.

Elijah Fenton

36 p. 151 *Olivia*: BAXTER is Richard Baxter (1615–91), a prolific author of pious works.

Gabriele D'Annunzio

37–40 p. 194 from *The Fresh-Water Venus*: CYPRIS is Venus; CNIDUS and COS were celebrated for the statues of Venus sculpted by Praxiteles: ILISSUS, a river in Attica; ACIDALIAN relates to the surname of Venus – Acidalia.

Anonymous

41 p. 204 This is a version, in aural circulation, of 'Lines on a Book Borrowed from the Ship's Doctor', composed by A. P. Herbert c.1927. See A. P. Herbert, *A.P.H., His Life and Times* (London, 1970).

Index of Poets

Index of First Lines

Richard Brautigan
Sombrero Fallout £1

A heart-broken American writer starts a story about a sombrero that falls out of the sky. But the story is discarded as he scours his apartment for strands of his departed Japanese girlfiend's hair. And in the wastebin, the sombrero story carries on without its author, growing into a national holocaust so great that only Norman Mailer can report its dimensions to the dumbfounded world: 'Hell,' he tells the nation, 'There is no other word for it . . .'

'Studded with wry surreal gags' NEW STATESMAN

Revenge of the Lawn £1

The sixty-two stories in this collection are vivid, delightfully informal, and mostly autobiographical. Fantasies, cameos and reminiscences of childhood in Tacoma, Washington and San Francisco.
In the short story, Brautigan shows himself to be a writer of wit, humanity and stunning originality. *Revenge of the Lawn* is a book as delicious in its humour and freshness as *Trout Fishing in America*.

The Abortion:
An Historical Romance 1966 £1.25

The Abortion is about the romantic possibilities of a public library in California – a library with a difference: one where authors can bring their manuscripts, 'the unwanted, the lyrical and haunted volumes of American writing'. Such volumes as *Growing Flowers by Candlelight in Hotel Rooms*, *My Trike* and *Love Always Beautiful*, a book rejected four hundred and fifty-nine times. Into this depository of dreams comes Vida, a girl with a Botticellian face and Playboy furniture legs, who spreads erotic confusion wherever she goes . . .

Martin Bax
The Hospital Ship 95p

Out of Martin Bax's astonishing vision of contemporary civilization in collapse sails *The Hospital Ship*, an atomic-powered ark attempting to salvage a 'remnant' from a world whose recent wars have resulted in the total loss of both social and individual stability. When the psychiatrist, Sir Maximov Flint, joins the ship he introduces his own extraordinary solution — love therapy. Savage violence, searing black comedy and a powerful vein of triumphant eroticism make this first novel an extraordinary, indeed a transforming experience.

'. . . the most exciting, stimulating and brilliantly conceived book I have read since Burroughs' novels' J. G. BALLARD

Renata Adler
Speedboat 90p

In scene after scene — at schools and college, covering news stories around the world, living in a brownstone in New York, listening to conversations at sea, in hospitals, at warfronts and parties, teaching at a city university, working on a political compaign — this brilliant first novel, about a woman journalist, creates a compelling vision of our time and conveys the feelings, thoughts, undertones, experiences, sad murmurs, voices and discontinuities of the way we live.

'An amazing writer of fiction' JOHN UPDIKE

Anita Loos
Gentlemen Prefer Blondes 50p

In 1925 a new kind of heroine burst upon the Jazz Age world: Lorelei Lee, a not-so-dumb, gold-digging blonde with a single-minded devotion to orchids, champagne and diamonds.

'I reclined on a sofa reading *Gentlemen Prefer Blondes* for three days. I am putting the piece in a place of honour' JAMES JOYCE

'Without hesitation, the best book on philosophy written by an American' GEORGE SANTAYANA

Ian McEwan
In Between the Sheets 90p

First Love, Last Rites, Ian McEwan's first volume of stories and winner of the 1976 Somerset Maugham Award, was rapturously received as the work of a brilliantly original new writer. Here now is his second collection, as dark, dangerous and funny as the first.

'The most exciting fiction writer in England under 30' PETER LEWIS, DAILY MAIL

'Exact, tender, funny, voluptuous, disturbing' THE TIMES

First Love, Last Rites £1.25

Under Ian McEwan's manipulations, depravity may take on the guise of innocence and butterflies can become sinister. With equal power, he can show a child's life become fouled by the macabre, or distil the awakening sensations of first love, tracing its ritual initiations and infusing them with a luxuriant sensual imagery.

'A brilliant performance, showing an originality astonishing for a writer still in his mid twenties' ANTHONY THWAITE, OBSERVER